Book 3, The Pet Bereavement Series

My Cat Is Dying: What Do I Do?

Navigating the Emotions, Decisions, and Options for Healing Pet Loss

Wendy Van de Poll, MS, CEOL

ISBN: 978-0-9973756-2-6

DISCLAIMER

If you are ever feeling like you can no longer function with your life, become suicidal, and any of the normal grief feelings have become extreme for you, then that is considered unhealthy grief. This is the time to call your hospital, medical practitioner, psychologist, or other health care provider that is trained to help you. Do not isolate yourself if you are experiencing unhealthy grief. Get the professional help that you require.

THANK YOU!

Thank you for purchasing *My Cat Is Dying: What Do I Do?* As a way of showing my appreciation, I have a gift for you: A Cat Grief Support Kit that you can use while reading this book.

To Download Your

FREE Cat Grief Support Kit

Please Go To:

https://www.centerforpetlossgrief.com/book-3-gift-sign-page

This book is dedicated to all the felines in my life—

Those that grace the people they live with, those that roam the wilds of nature and show up on my path, and those that visit me in my visions and dreams.

You grace my life with magic, healing, and wisdom.

Contents

Introduction

What do you do when you get the news your cat has a life-threatening illness? Are you feeling numb with shock? Are you in a state of panic from the sudden overwhelm?

Realistically, what are you going to do? She is your best friend, and you can't imagine what life would be like without her sweet meows, gentle nuzzles, and heart vibrating purrs that fill your soul with delight.

Your veterinarian gave you the news that your beloved kitty is reaching the end of her life. You are beyond belief, and you say to yourself, "My cat is dying . . . What am I going to do?"

This book will offer tools to support you with your grief and will guide you on how to stay present through the muck of caretaking your terminally ill cat. In this book, I supply you with options, so you can begin to heal your pet grief during this difficult yet very special time. I will support you right away on your pet grief journey.

This book is for you if you received news that your cat is going to die, time is limited, and you want to do the best you can to support your cat through this particular time during their cycle of life. This book is also for you if you know and understand that your relationship with your cat is unique and exceptional.

My Cat Is Dying: What Do I Do? has been designed just for you. It is your emotional emergency first-aid kit that will support you through the rollercoaster ride that you are about to take.

It is your handbook and journal to always keep with you, packed with useful information. Consider it your new best friend.

My Cat Is Dying: What Do I Do? will be there for you always, supporting you as a close friend to walk with you on the journey of pet loss grief with unconditional love.

Something special I'm offering you that I've not found in other pet grief books are contemplation questions. At the end of each chapter, you will find three *Contemplation Questions*, designed to help you proceed even more deeply on your grief journey to become an active participant when coping with your cat's illness.

With years of experience of supporting people as their cats go from the physical to the spiritual realm I have gained a tremendous amount of wisdom and knowledge concerning the soul of the cat. Our cats have a unique view of the world and of us. And when we listen to their voice, they can have a profound effect on the way we as humans approach life.

Along with my personal experiences with cats, plus being a certified end-of-life and pet loss grief coach (CEOL), as well as a licensed massage therapist for humans, horses, hounds, and, at times, cats, I have helped countless people around the world to feel safe with their feelings of grief and have a compassionate outlet to express what they are feeling.

People who feel alone with their feelings of grief when their cats are reaching the end of their lives have found support from the suggestions and information in this helpful book.

Sasha, whose cat Louie suffered kidney failure, explained—

This book is written with kindness and love, which is just what I needed when going through such a difficult time with Louis. I could dive right in and get the support and guidance I needed. There in the book are Wendy's words to help you understand and deal with feelings of grief and to help you make the most of the time with your cat. This book helps ensure you are doing everything to care for them and to celebrate their life, and her words will help you heal.

The case studies showed me that others have been through what I am going through, and they found a way to live through it and even experience moments of joy. I also liked the "Contemplation Questions" at the end of each chapter, which gave me a chance to explore my feelings and understand that they are normal for me. One of the toughest things about saying good-bye to my cat was knowing when would be the right time to let go. Wendy helps you figure this out and provides guidance on final day preparation. This is such a difficult subject, but Wendy writes with apparent understanding.

I promise you that when you read and follow the tips in this book, you will feel like you have acquired a new best friend who totally gets what you are going through. And I promise it will be your first-aid kit that will give you solutions to some of the most difficult decisions and situations that you will experience.

Please don't be the person who goes through this difficult time of loss alone. Be the person who actively takes death by the hand. Be the person who can make sound decisions on how to take care of your cat during this special time. And be the person who looks at the pet loss grief journey not as an opportunity to fear death but as a journey to learn, love, grow, and heal.

The book that you are about to read will help you create a compassionate, respectful, healthy, and loving journey for you and your cat to share during this tough, yet unique, time.

Remember—you will never have to feel alone with your pet loss grief again!

CREATING YOUR JOURNEY
SECTION ONE

Where there is love there is life.

—Mahatma Gandhi

1. Receiving Grief

Having a cat in your life is part heartening and part mystical. Many don't understand how much cats can offer and enrich our lives. Unfortunately some think cats are only about being fiercely independent and non-communicative.

Being a cat-lover, you know cats can teach us about boundaries, self-reliance, and unconditional love. When we grace our lives with our feline friends and open our hearts to their voices, they will teach us amazing things about ourselves.

So, if it happens that you receive news that your cat only has a short period of time to live, your new and unexpected emotions are going to suddenly create chaos in your life—right now you may be feeling extreme anxiety or sadness. You may be unsure of what to do next—how to care for your cat and how to care for yourself.

You may be asking yourself, "Does it ever get easier with my pet loss grief?" The answer is no. However, by understanding what grief is and by employing the other great tools and support offered in this book, you are going to find that you are not alone. You are going to navigate this journey with respect and love, both for your cat and yourself.

You can now consider this book a new ally that will guide you and walk the journey of pet loss grief with you. I will help you understand what normal grief is and how you can begin to cope with it in this opening chapter.

If you are feeling hopeless right now because you don't know whom to talk to, how to get help, or whom to get help from— you are experiencing normal grief. This book will help you find support.

If your blood is starting to boil because you are so angry that your best friend is sick and you are feeling guilty, depressed, numb, or even shock—you are experiencing normal pet grief, and the tools in this book will help you.

Once you understand what normal grief is and what the expectations are for your grief experience, your journey will be different. It will become more manageable, so you can be more emotionally available to your cat in their final days.

Case Study — Sasha and Louie

When Sasha got the news that her ten-year-old calico cat, named Louie, was diagnosed with renal failure, she was distraught and overwhelmed. When she contacted me through my Shoulder to Lean On program, it had been four days since she'd received the news, and she hadn't slept, eaten, or talked to anyone. When she finally started calling everyone that she could think of to help her with the news, Sasha found herself terribly frustrated and hurt. Her friends and family didn't understand what she was going through and were impatient with her.

In our first conversation, Sasha was troubled, worried, and flustered. She was so confused that she jumped from one story to the next—never finishing a complete thought when she was explaining the situation to me. She cried unrestrainedly, had bouts of anger mixed with laughing uncontrollably, and, at times, was totally quiet, unable to articulate what she was feeling.

Now here is the thing—Sasha was having a healthy reaction to the news that Louie was sick. Sasha was experiencing *normal* pet loss grief.

I know that sounds weird, but this is how it works: the fact that Sasha could outwardly express herself to someone, who was non-judgmental and could listen to what she had to say without adding advice or suggestions, is what helped Sasha understand and cope with her grief, which, in turn, made her grief experience *normal*.

Just to clarify, even though Sasha's grief was normal, that didn't mean it was easy or short-lived. Sasha was feeling weird about her feelings and not comfortable about what was going on in her mind, in her body, and with her spiritual beliefs. And this is part of the natural, but uncomfortable, grief experience.

Sasha experienced a huge amount of guilt after she got the news. She felt guilty about not spending more time with Louie when he was younger. Sasha had a job that took her away from home a lot, so she would leave Louie for weeks with a pet sitter. This made her feel horrible about herself. Again, feeling such guilt is heart-twisting but also—normal.

In our conversation, I encouraged Sasha to talk about everything that she was feeling and going through—all the feelings that were driving her crazy and how she was going to begin to share this news with others.

The result—Sasha began to make sense of the myriad feelings and physical sensations that she was experiencing. She began to understand that what she was going through was very difficult but also—normal.

Plus, she learned that her original expectation—that she could avoid feeling grief—was not realistic. When this expectation changed and she realized that grief was healthy, she felt much better.

Over the course of our working together in my Shoulder to Lean On program, Sasha learned that her experiences of pet grief were difficult and uncomfortable but, at the same time, natural, healthy, and special.

By understanding her feelings and accepting those crazy thoughts, sensations, and spiritual upheavals, she began to walk the journey of losing Louie with respect for herself. This, in turn, gave her the direction and focus she needed to be present for her cat, Louie, and to give back to Louie the perfect gift—absolute love.

When our conversation for that day ended, Sasha wasn't free of feeling grief. Yet, she had more strength and grounding to move forward to contemplate her next moment in this special journey.

Element 1 — Normal and Necessary

What Sasha's story demonstrates is that the first thing to know about pet grief is that what you are feeling and thinking, though uncomfortable and difficult, is also normal and healthy. Grief is necessary, so it is critical that you let your feelings happen.

If you stuff grief down, so many negative things can happen to your health and well-being. It will negatively affect how you live from the day you receive the news, how you begin to move forward, and how well you are able to be present and supportive to your cat in their final days.

In fact, if you stuff your feelings down, your normal grief feelings could transform into unhealthy grief feelings and actions. We will talk about unhealthy grief later in this chapter.

Normal Grief Feelings — A List

Here are some normal feelings of pet grief that you may be experiencing now or later in your journey.

- *Physical* ~ crying, sobbing, wailing, numbness, dry mouth, nausea, tightness in chest, restlessness, fatigue, sleep disturbance, appetite disturbance, dizziness, fainting, or shortness of breath

- *Intellectual* ~ sense of unreality, inability to concentrate, feeling preoccupied by the loss, hallucinations concerning the loss, a sense that time is passing very slowly, or a desire to rationalize feelings about the loss

- *Emotional* ~ anger, depression, guilt, anxiety, relief, irritability, desire to blame others about the loss, self-doubt, lowered self-esteem, feeling overwhelmed, or feeling out of control, hopeless, or helpless

- *Social* ~ feelings of isolation or alienation, feeling rejected by others, or feeling reluctant to ask for help

- *Spiritual* ~ feeling angry at your deity when a loss occurs or bargaining with your deity to prevent loss

A Life of Its Own

As you can see, normal grief comes in many shapes and sizes. The thing about grief is that it has a life of its own.

What this means is that you can be going through a quiet period of your journey where you are feeling relatively good. Then something happens, and it triggers intense, and perhaps unexpected, feelings of pet grief.

I am here to tell you to let this happen. Let the feelings course through your body. Let them rage. Let your tears flow. It's healthy and necessary.

Abnormal Grief Feelings

Yet, if you are ever feeling like you can no longer function with your life, if you become suicidal and any of the normal grief feelings become extreme, then that is considered unhealthy grief. This is the time to call your hospital, medical practitioner, psychologist, or other healthcare provider who is trained to help you. Do not isolate yourself if you are experiencing unhealthy grief. Get the professional help that you require.

When your feelings are healthy and you are letting them happen, I can assure you that you will be more present to take care of your cat. You will do amazing things for your cat and yourself (something I'll go into in greater detail in chapter 7).

Element 2 — Reach Out

In addition to recognizing your normal grief feelings, a second essential component for navigating your pet grief journey is to reach out to someone else, as Sasha did. Look for someone who will listen to every word you express with respect and compassion, and share your grief experience with this person. In doing this, you will feel better about what you are going through, you will feel supported, and you will come to better understand your own grief.

Element 3 — Time with Your Cat

Spend time with your cat, as Sasha did with Louie. She made sure that she spent quality time with him every day, without distraction. Since she had a close bond with Louie, she knew exactly what he loved. By brushing him, playing with the laser pointer, and feeding him special treats that he loved, Sasha was consciously healing her feelings of guilt and providing joy to Louie at the same time.

Element 4 — Familiarize Yourself

Also, get to know your grief. Become a friend to your grief. You are going to be spending a lot of time with your feelings over the next few days, months, and even years, so embrace your feelings.

Spend some time responding to the *Contemplation Questions* at the end of this chapter. These questions will help guide you to recognize your own unique feelings of normal pet grief.

Chapter Wrap-Up

Having a terminally ill cat is certainly hard. Your cat is your special companion. You have shared many beautiful moments together. When your cat reaches the end of their life, it demands that you be present for them. This experience can change your life.

The first twenty-four hours is the time for you to just be in the moment by breathing and preparing yourself for the journey to come. Revisit the four elements I've given you in this chapter and begin to internalize them and act upon them. Respond to the chapter's *Contemplation Questions* to help you manage your normal, but uncomfortable, feelings of grief.

In the next chapter, you will learn how having goals and checklists will help you through this special time. I am also going to share with you the checklist that I give my clients to help you to create your own unique list.

Chapter One Contemplation Questions

1. What did you do in the first twenty-four hours of getting the news that your cat is terminally ill? How did you take care of yourself and your cat?

2. Now that you know what the feelings of normal grief are, can you list all the feelings of pet grief that you are going through?

3. Are you having any abnormal feelings of grief? Which ones? If so, do you have your healthcare practitioner's contact information readily available? List the phone number/s here.

2. Crafting Your Plan

As you already know, it is important for you to be there for your cat right now. Yet, you may be feeling disordered and confused with the news, and it's hard for you to have optimistic and encouraging thoughts.

You may even feel a little helpless about not knowing the best thing you can do for your cat. Defeat and hopelessness may be setting in, and that can be causing you more stress and grief.

Your emotions are up and down. There are so many things that need to be taken care of, and you don't know where to begin.

A Personalized Record

The solution—a checklist. You will design a checklist with both your goals and the personality of your cat in mind. It will help you move through your day with your cat with a whole lot more love and a whole lot less chaos.

You will discover that by creating goals and checklists, you will actually stay more focused on your and your cat's needs. The goals and checklists will guide you through your grief to help you stay dedicated to the tasks at hand.

The beautiful thing about creating a checklist is that it will also trigger some heartfelt memories that you share with your cat. When this happens, you can spend time reflecting on the memories, something we will cover in a later chapter.

This is a trying time, and your emotions can zap your energy. Without a checklist you can forget things, be disorganized, and not be prepared for important decisions and events that may pop up.

Creating a checklist that is designed with your goals in mind will help you make decisions, choose veterinarians, and be the best advocate you can be for your cat. This checklist will be your customized strategy to guide you on how to purposefully live your life now that your cat is sick.

Now, that is not to say that by having a checklist you will not experience grief or that having a plan will make your grief any less important. Instead, a checklist will guide you every day to stay focused on how to provide the best care for your cat and yourself.

My clients love their lists. They find that their checklists are essential for daily stability. Some even consider their checklists as part of their support teams, which we will talk about more in a later chapter.

Case Study — Chloe and Cha-Cha

Chloe's cat, Cha-Cha, was dying of a spinal tumor, and Chloe was overcome with vast amounts of grief. When she called me, she had just gotten the news the day before and was so confused about what to do. She confided to me, "Wendy, I am literally walking in circles in my living room. I have so many things going on in my mind."

Because Chloe was so distressed, I had her make her checklist right away while we were talking on our first call. I had her list every task that she could think of that needed to be done.

I then had her make copies of the checklist and post them all over her house (in the bathroom too) and even in her car, so she could conveniently access them. Every morning when Chloe got up, she would look at her checklist for the day and circle the things that she wanted to accomplish.

I explained to her that her list was available whenever she needed support. She could look at it when she was feeling grief, when she wanted to clear her mind, or when she wanted to give Cha-Cha her total attention.

It was a little difficult for Chloe to focus to make her list, but she emailed me the next day with a copy of her complete list. It was amazing. She had so many wonderful things on it— things that she wanted to do with Cha-Cha, self-care for herself, weekly and monthly visits and calls to her veterinarian, medication times, feeding times, play times, and everything else that she wanted to accomplish.

Yet, Chloe was being extremely critical of herself and her list. She felt as if she didn't have enough on her list. She was experiencing anxiety because she was concerned that it took time to accomplish some tasks and wanted to have them all completed immediately.

I explained to her, "Chloe, this is part of the grief rollercoaster that you are going to experience. This time that you have left with Cha-Cha is going to test your patience. Keep that in mind when you feel like you are getting ahead of yourself. Grief loves to test patience."

When she remembered to pace herself with the goals that she'd set out to do and when she remembered that she didn't have to do them all in one afternoon, Chloe calmed the chaos and opened up space for peace and presence of mind in her daily life. She was then able to spend more quality time with Cha-Cha.

Chloe learned to love her checklist very quickly. It helped her stay focused on how she was going to live her life while taking care of Cha-Cha. Her list provided her with a less chaotic mind and a sense of relief that she wouldn't forget something important.

After Cha-Cha reached the end of her life, Chloe revealed to me—

> *I was so distraught when I got the news about Cha-Cha. She was healthy until one day she couldn't get up. My mind was going in so many different directions I didn't know where to focus. When you had me get those important tasks organized, I felt so much better. Getting my daily tasks out of my mind and on paper gave me a sense of control that when my grief was raging, I could look at my list, do a task, and then give my cat a huge hug. My list was a lifesaver during my last few weeks with Cha-Cha.*

The List

As with Chloe, I have my clients create a main list of everything they want to do, as soon as they can, to care for their cats and themselves. In my Hand to Hold and Shoulder to Lean On programs, we do this during our first appointment or soon after.

To make your list, you will use the *Contemplation Questions* at the end of this chapter to identify the particular activities that you want to do for your cat and yourself. That way, you can name the items that are personal to your circumstances and your cat's needs. Once you've created this customized list, you can then download the more general "master list" that I've created. You can download that list at the beginning of this book.

This is Your Cat Grief Support Kit, which includes other gifts as well to be used throughout this book.

After you make your own list, take a look at the "master list" that I created for you. Feel free to combine the two lists into a single, customized strategic checklist that reflects the plans and needs of you and your cat on your unique pet loss grief journey.

Once you've made your long and full strategic checklist, you can then draw from it to make daily to-do lists, delineating what you want to do for yourself and your cat on a daily basis. This way, you can keep your long-term plans in mind (via the full strategic checklist) as you plan out each day. And with a daily checklist of plans, even when unexpected waves of grief hit you, you have a plan that will remind you to care for yourself and your cat.

This might sound tedious, but once you do it, you have it. The goal of these lists is to help you stay focused, centered, and supported. Have a copy of your strategic checklist always available as a reference, so every day you can choose the activities that you want to do.

Many of my clients do weekly, rather than daily, lists, so they can plan ahead (an example is included in Your Cat Grief

Support Kit). Yet, on some days, everyone finds value in creating a daily list because it allows for more detail.

Here is an example of a day in Chloe's checklist. She didn't feel it was necessary to include times. Even though there is an order to this list and you see duplicate activities, Chloe didn't feel that it was always necessary to follow the exact order. Chloe's daily list helped her to stay focused, to keep her anxiety from taking over her life, and to remember to take care of herself.

One of Chloe's Daily Lists

Eat Breakfast

Hand-feed Cha-Cha

Give Cha-Cha medication

Brush Cha-Cha

Do email

Work on stuff for appointment with Wendy

Call work

Run and go to gym

Call Susan (friend)

Call holistic/cancer vet

Snuggle on the bed with Cha-Cha

Research holistic care for Cha-Cha

Schedule massage for me

Cook dinner for both Cha-Cha and me

Give Cha-Cha medication

Read on the couch with Cha-Cha

Meditate

Give Cha-Cha medication

Bed

As with all my clients, I encourage you to make photocopies of your list and post the copies in various places—the refrigerator, the computer, the bathroom mirror, the glove compartment in your car—anywhere that you'll be able to see it frequently throughout the day.

It's important to know that these lists can and will change as your days progress with your cat.

You will probably add new things weekly, maybe even daily, to your list. Consider your checklist a really good friend guiding you through this journey. Lists provide great ways to stay focused on the task at hand.

Some Dos and Don'ts

Sometimes people will experience their pet grief by feeling as if they have to do everything on their lists perfectly and every day. This is how Chloe felt initially. And just as Chloe learned, you may also learn that even though that is a common feeling when experiencing grief, it is important to pace yourself.

It's important to remember that even though you have a checklist, you must spend quality time with your cat. You want every day to count and matter.

You want to remember every single moment that you have with your cat. You want to create a time for your cat to feel super comfortable and taken care of.

Without a checklist, the distractions that you have in your everyday life can take over. Then at the end of the day, you realize you didn't spend the time that you wanted with your cat or you forgot something important. Then you feel guilty, which then creates more stress and chaos in your life.

Making your checklist and setting daily goals will provide you with a way to navigate through, around, and amidst stress and chaos. Your checklist allows you to do things that matter most quickly.

The checklist is a great tool for helping you cope with your pet loss. It will help you stay focused on your cat rather than the mind clutter, which can lead to anxiety. This mind clutter will take you away from being present in the final days, weeks, or months that your cat has left to live.

Please use the three *Contemplation Questions* at the end of the chapter in conjunction with the general "master list" that you can find in Your Cat Grief Support Kit to create your customized strategic checklist.

Chapter Wrap-Up

A unique checklist is a great tool for helping you cope with pet grief. It helps you stay focused on your cat's needs, as well as your own, rather than allowing your mind clutter to take over, which can then lead to anxiety and chaos.

In chapter 3, I am going to teach you about the seven stages of grief when coping with pet loss. With each of these stages, I am going to give you examples of what you can expect from people. Plus, I'll teach you how to heal yourself in this journey so that you are ready to deal with whatever comes your way.

Chapter Two Contemplation Questions

1. What are your goals for this special time? Include any new activities that involve you and your cat, and you alone—feeding schedule, exercise times, self-care, care for your cat, veterinarian visits, and anything else that you can think of.

2. Along with the checklist that I provided you in Your Cat Grief Support Kit and the list you made above, can you create your own strategic checklist that includes your unique goals?

3. What are the particular things that you would like to include on your list that reflect the personality of your cat?

3. Grasping Your Grief and Loss Stages

If you are feeling a little raw with your emotions of grief, that is okay and natural. As I've already shared, grief has a life of its own. Know that what you are going through is common, natural, and normal. Your sorrow, apprehension, uncertainty, and anger are okay and healthy to feel. Yet, there is more to your journey of coping with the fact that your cat is terminally ill.

Pet loss grief actually has seven identifiable stages. By understanding these seven stages, your confusion and possible terror about what you and your cat are experiencing can change to give you greater peace. Learning which stage of pet loss grief you are experiencing is extremely helpful for your coping and healing journey. You can gain compassion and respect for your unique experience, both of which are vital.

Living with a cat that has been diagnosed with a life-threatening illness can be an excursion in its own right. Your daily life of caring for your cat will change from moment to moment. You want to do the best you can for your beloved companion and for yourself.

No matter what emotions you are experiencing while you are caring for your cat, one of the most important things to remember is to cherish the life you are having with them right now! And that includes understanding the stage of grief that you are in.

The grief that you are feeling is a given. It is there, and it's not going to go away. Yet, it will change as time progresses. You will become more and more involved with creating the best life you possibly can for your cat. Because your focus will be on your cat, you might forget to listen to your emotions.

The Seven Stages of Grief

It is extremely helpful to know not only what normal grief is but also what the normal stages of grief are.

Dr. Elisabeth Kubler-Ross was a pioneer in the hospice movement. While she wasn't a pet grief person, what she discovered can be applied to the passage of pet grief.

In 1969, in her book *On Death and Dying*, Dr. Kubler-Ross made the five steps of grief and/or death well-known. These five steps covered the stages of grieving for the death of a loved one:

1. Denial

2. Anger

3. Bargaining

4. Depression

5. Acceptance

These five stages became very popular and are used widely, mostly during the dying process. However, people working in this field began to expand on her various philosophies and standards. Currently there are seven stages of grief:

1. Shock and Denial

2. Pain and Guilt

3. Anger and Bargaining

4. Depression, Reflection, and Loneliness

5. Adjustment to Life

6. Your New Normal

7. Acceptance and Hope

These are the seven stages of grief that I use in my practice when helping people like you explore their grief and loss stages in regard to pet loss. Over and over my clients tell me that knowing this valuable information now rather than later prepares them even more fully for the future. You too can expect that these stages will guide you to a deeper understanding of what you are experiencing with your feelings.

Keep in mind that since your journey is your journey, you may not experience all of these stages as your daily pet loss experience progresses. Yet, you may.

Whatever you experience is natural, so be compassionate with yourself about what you are going through. Never compare your experience to someone else's because grief isn't experienced in exactly the same way by all people. It is a unique and special journey that you are undergoing.

Case Study — Heather, Tuxedo, and the Seven Stages

Heather, a client of mine, experienced all seven stages of grief. Not only that, but also she experienced all seven stages in their exact order. When she received news that her cat, Tuxedo, had jaw cancer, Heather emailed me. She was stunned and just couldn't believe it was true.

Stage One: Shock and Denial

As we worked together, Heather began to deny the prognosis and believed that it was really not happening to Tuxedo. Her cat didn't have jaw cancer, and there must have been a mistake. She kept repeating, "This is not true, it can't be. I have fed Tuxedo organic food all of her life, and she is healthy. She can't have cancer—the doctors are wrong."

Stage Two: Pain and Guilt

Heather was feeling extreme agony. She felt wounded and was confused about how she truly felt at this time. I assured her that this was customary and the second stage of grief.

When the news started to lose its newness and when the reality and certainty of the situation became apparent, Heather's self-blame became more and more intense. She went through feelings of guilt and remorse that maybe she had caused the cancer. She felt as if she should have done something differently when Tuxedo was younger—different veterinarian, different food, different treats, different environment.

Stage Three: Anger and Bargaining

Then Heather got really angry at herself and at the disease. She began to bargain and ask her higher power to give her a sign on how to cure the cancer.

Heather became so angry that the disturbing disease was killing Tuxedo. She wanted it gone, to go away and never return again. She started to hate herself because she believed she caused the cancer. She felt full responsibility, and her rage was incalculable.

One day when Heather couldn't stuff her anger down any longer, she went into her bedroom and yelled as loudly as she could into a pillow. She cried, screamed, and yelled. She asked her higher power not to let Tuxedo die and promised all kinds of things if only Tuxedo could be healed.

Stage Four: Depression, Reflection, and Loneliness

When Heather began to understand that anger and bargaining were part of the journey, she then began to feel rundown, dejected, and lonesome.

She found herself having intense episodes of weeping, shock, and overwhelming feelings of depression. She told me, "I have no one in my family that understands how important Tuxedo is to me." Every day she felt as if she were totally alone and isolated within her grief.

As we continued to work together, Heather began to see that her feelings of depression and loneliness were part of the process. Soon she was able to reflect on the life that she still had with Tuxedo.

She said to me, "Even though I have strong feelings of grief every day, I acknowledge these feelings as healthy and necessary. Now that I understand this, I am able to experience the life I still have with Tuxedo. I am grateful you helped me with this because, otherwise, I would not be available for Tuxedo's needs."

Stage Five: Adjustment to Life

At first it was difficult for Heather to recognize stage five. With Tuxedo being sick and her life changing drastically, Heather wanted to hold on to what was familiar in her life.

She confided one day, "My goodness, this is tough, Wendy. I have felt shock, denial, pain, guilt, anger, depression, and loneliness. I have even been outrageously irritated at my higher power and tried bargaining with them to help Tuxedo. Now, I have to adapt to a change I don't want. It's not that I don't want the best for Tuxedo, but how do I navigate this change and feel good about it?"

This was a powerful question for Heather. Throughout this book, we will be talking about adjusting to a new life in more detail. Yet, for now, keep in mind that this period is about integrating these changes into your daily life to make it work for you and your cat.

Stage Six: Your New Normal

As time moved on, Heather began to adjust to the changes. She found that she needed to stay home more and not go out with friends. Heather wanted to be with Tuxedo as much as she could, and it didn't bother her that she had to stop going out after work or stop going on long hikes on the weekends.

She even discovered who her true friends really were. There were two friends in particular that supported Heather and helped her deal with the changes in her life. They loved Tuxedo as well, so instead of going hiking on weekends together, they had picnic lunches in Heather's yard every Saturday with Tuxedo in attendance.

Stage Seven: Acceptance and Hope

When Heather began to experience the last stage of pet grief, she was ready to move forward with an entirely different attitude. She accepted the fact that Tuxedo was going to die.

She had found her new normal and had her plan of action on how she was going to take care of Tuxedo—what food, what doctors, what new ways she could spend quality time with Tuxedo. Now Heather could live every day with her with the hope and desire to do the best she could with the care that Tuxedo needed.

This was the stage when Heather became more aware and accepted her grief stages. She was confident that she could provide everything that Tuxedo needed. It became easier to make decisions in whatever stage of grief she was experiencing.

Chapter Wrap-Up

These stages provide references to guide you on how you can process your pet loss while still caring for your cat. Heather experienced all seven stages in the exact order. By no means do you need to experience them all or experience them in the exact order as Heather did.

Use the three *Contemplative Questions* at the end of this chapter to help guide you with your unique stages of grief.

Again, please remember that you are not alone on your grief journey. There are others who are experiencing tremendous grief due to pet loss just as you are.

In the next chapter, I am going to teach you about the myths that surround pet grief and how these myths can hold you back from having a healthy relationship with your cat. I am also going to show you how you can turn these myths around so that they can help you on your journey.

Chapter Three Contemplation Questions

1. What stage of grief are you in right now?

2. How many stages of grief have you experienced and what have you learned about your unique journey through each of these stages?

3. Wendy helps her clients know and understand the seven stages of pet grief early in their journeys. Her clients find that by knowing this valuable information early on, rather than later, they are better prepared for the future. In what ways does knowing this information now help you prepare for your future?

4. Debunking the Myths

Now that you have an understanding of normal grief (chapter 1) and have explored the seven stages of grief (chapter 3), we are now going to visit the multitude of myths that often accompany pet grief. To introduce the myths, let's return to Sasha, whom I supported in her grief journey with Louie.

Myth Confrontation

My client Sasha, on our second call, started the conversation with intense anger, then started to laugh and giggle about a comment that one of her "best" friends said, "Sasha, you are being ridiculous. Louie is a cat for, goodness sakes. Move on and just get another cat—put Louie out of his misery."

Sasha couldn't believe how insensitive her friend was being and felt really angry at her. Sasha's anger was so intense that she told me, "I can't be friends with this person anymore!" After she said that, she started crying about it, and then she started to laugh uncontrollably. Then she became horrified that she was laughing. Sasha told me that she realized it was really wrong of her to feel any joy during this time of Louie's illness and that she was confused by her emotions.

My response—"Sasha, that's just a grief myth. Don't you believe it. You are going to live out a variety of emotions on your grief journey. And, at times, joy will be one of those feelings, and it is perfectly natural."

With my guidance, Sasha did not stuff her emotions down. She allowed the laughter and the tears to come. In doing so, she really felt relief. She was able to breathe and understand that laughing was another way to express her grief. She felt as if a substantial block had been lifted from her heart.

In debunking the "no joy during grieving" myth, Sasha finished her session feeling a lot stronger on her journey. With renewed confidence and greater clarity, she understood that she could be the best caretaker for Louie.

Myths about grieving, like the one Sasha voiced, have been around for a long time, and they can either really help you with your grief or be a hindrance to your healing process. The key to making these myths help is to be aware of them and debunk them.

You will find a copy of these myths in Your Cat Grief Support Kit that you downloaded at the beginning of this book.

The Myths

1. *It is selfish and extravagant to mourn and grieve the death of a cat when our world has so much human suffering.*

Debunking—You are a cat-lover, and you understand how important your fury friend is to you. The grief surrounding the fact that your cat has a terminal illness is significant.

People are capable of simultaneously grieving both animals and humans. One doesn't have to detract from the other. By grieving and mourning your cat, you are showing tremendous compassion for the universe as a whole. Feeling compassion opens you to feeling more compassion. A compassion that starts because of your cat grows, deepens, and blooms into a great compassion for all creatures, including humans. It is a gift that keeps on giving. Compassion and love are always good things.

2.You must follow the seven stages of grief in their exact order so that you can truly heal your pain.

Debunking—Grief is not about following a prescribed list. Grief is tenacious and can really dig into your daily routine, which can render you feeling hopeless.

The last thing that you need to be worried about is following the seven stages of grief in a particular order. Although the stages of grief are extremely valuable, the order in which you experience them is variable. Let the stages unfold naturally.

3. There is a right and wrong way to grieve.

Debunking—As with following the seven stages of grief in chronological order, the same is true about your unique grief experience.

Your relationship with your cat is special. No two people grieve the same way. Grief manifests itself in various ways and frequently changes. While one person may feel sadness, another person may feel anger about the news. Your grief journey is yours and very unique.

Grieving is very personal and individual to your experience with your cat. It depends on your personality, the personality of your cat, the nature of their illness, your spiritual beliefs, and your coping style. Understand that your journey is special, and respect the journey.

4. The best thing to do is to grieve and mourn alone, especially because it is just a cat.

Debunking—We have been taught that in order to be strong and independent we should not share our grief. It would burden others and be inappropriate to let them know how we are feeling.

On the contrary, it is important to reach out to others. Even still, you will want to protect yourself from being judged for loving and taking care of your cat.

Take your time with choosing whom you can turn to for support because some people don't understand or take pet loss seriously. Find a support group, pet loss coach, and/or friend that will allow you to talk about your grief without making you feel crazy or weird. We cover this more in chapter 9.

Remember, if there ever comes a time when you can no longer function in life, please see the appropriate healthcare provider.

5. You have to be "strong" with your grief.

Debunking—In general our society teaches that grief feelings can be a sign of weakness especially in regard to having a cat that is terminally ill.

Feeling sad, frightened, lonely, or depressed are all normal reactions. Crying doesn't mean that you are weak.

Let yourself feel the emotions, physical sensations, and spiritual challenges that you are going through. There is reason for you to have these feelings. Plus, there is no reason why you need to feel that you have to "protect" your family or friends by being "strong."

Showing your feelings will help you and may even help them.

6. Grief will always feel the same and shouldn't take long to deal with.

Debunking—Never! And that is okay. Our grief changes as each day goes by. You will never forget your cat. Yet, your feelings of grief will change.

Never feel like you have to rush through your grief journey. It takes time. Patience comes in handy when you are in the beginning stages of grief.

The goal for healing your pet loss is not to "get over it." We never stop feeling grief for losing a pet. But we learn to move forward in life again with fond memories.

7. No one gets pet grief, so you are alone with what you are going through.

Debunking—You are never alone with the grief that you are going through. It may feel like that at times because many people don't know what it feels like to get the news that their cat is going to die. They just don't understand what you are going through.

People (even cat-lovers) will say unsupportive things, for example, "There are so many cats that need homes. See this as an opportunity to give another cat a needed home!" or "At least it wasn't a child."

Even still, there are many, many people who do know the grief you are experiencing. It just may take some time to find the right people in your life to support you in a healthy way. There are supportive friends, end-of-life and grief coaches, and pet loss support groups to walk the journey with you. We will talk about this more in chapter 9.

Remember—you are not alone with your pet loss grief.

8. Pet loss grief will go away on its own.

Debunking—Many of my clients call me when they have just gotten the news that their cat is going to die. They feel a tremendous amount of grief and just want it to go away.

It takes work to heal your pet loss grief. To feel more comfortable, take your time. Be an active participant so that you can experience the stages of grief.

Your cat is certainly special to you. It is a really important to let your emotions happen and to experience them. If you feel like they will go away on their own, you are only stuffing them in.

And as many of my clients say, "Grief has a great talent of surprising you when you least expect it." It is better to actively acknowledge, process, and experience it than to stuff it down only for it to pop up at surprising, very unwelcoming times in unanticipated ways.

9. Once you do all the grief work, it will go away.

Debunking—Once you do all the work in your grieving process, remember that grief can come up again. It is not uncommon to have deep feelings of grief show up again, even years later. It is normal for this to happen.

Grief never goes away, and that is okay. Many of my clients report that when their grief shows up after a few months or years, they are happy about it because it gives them a chance to say, "I love you," to their cats that died.

For now, since you just got the news, tuck this thought in a special place, so you'll know what to expect later.

10. Having feelings of joy at times when your cat is terminally ill is not good.

Debunking—Here is the thing—you just got devastating news that your beloved companion is going to die. Your cat is sick, and maybe the vet determined that they only have one week to live.

The last thing that you probably think you are allowed to feel is joyful or happy. In fact, you probably are feeling many emotions from this news, and that is okay.

But it is also okay to experience moments of joy, even when you are grieving about your cat's illness. It is healthy and doesn't mean you are forgetting your cat's situation.

Moments of joy are normal. They mean that your body is giving you a breather from the stress, pain, anxiety, and sadness. Joy is a natural response and a survival mechanism that allows healing.

11. It is horrible to feel happy or relieved that your cat died.

Debunking—You may feel that it is a little early to talk about this myth, but I believe that it is important for you to be prepared for it now.

Being prepared will remind you that when the time comes when your cat reaches the end of their life, it is okay to feel relieved and even slightly glad.

This is a very common feeling for my clients that suffered the pain and angst of losing their cats to terminal illnesses. When your cat is in pain and suffering every day, it can take a lot out of you emotionally, physically, and spiritually. It breaks your heart and can leave you feeling hopeless and helpless.

At your cat's death, feeling slightly glad, relieved, and even ashamed are also very normal feelings of grief. Keep in mind that it is not a selfish feeling but a feeling that your cat is no longer suffering in the physical world.

The Other Side of the Myths: Grace and Compassion

These myths are very common, and many people think they are true. These myths, in conjunction with the inappropriate comments that people make (more on these in chapter 5) can easily trigger your grief. If you are not aware of them, you can become confused as to why suddenly you are feeling sad or very angry.

Even though they may be well-meaning friends, family, or co-workers, when one of them offers you a myth as a so-called "word of wisdom," it can pack a powerful punch to trigger your pet loss grief. However, once you become aware of these myths and why they are not true, you will be able to react to them with grace and compassion for yourself and your beloved companion.

Here is the thing about believing these myths and letting them affect you—I have seen in my practice that when folks believe and live by these myths, they get stuck with their grief and have a difficult time gaining personal calm.

When they learn to take these myths, debunk them, and replace them with positive thoughts and actions, they are able to spend more time loving their cats, rather than being stressed out with unknown anxiety or other feelings of grief that they may be experiencing.

Please revisit these myths and the debunking of them. It will help prepare you for the multitude of thoughts and feelings that you will have and the comments people will make.

Use the three *Contemplative Questions* at the end of this chapter to help you to identify and then change any myths that you may encounter in your journey.

Plus, with Your Cat Grief Support Kit that you downloaded at the beginning of this book, you can stay aware of the common myths and the easy debunking of them. Feel free to print out the list of common myths and post it on the bathroom mirror, your desk, and the refrigerator. Post this list anywhere so that it is readily available when you want to revisit it.

Chapter Wrap-Up

Myths about pet loss grief can be roadblocks to moving forward with meaning and purpose in regard to the bond you have with your pet.

The way to remove the roadblock and make the myths work for you is to be aware of them, debunk them, and then find something positive in them.

To repeat, always remember—you are not alone on your grief journey. There are others that are experiencing the same thing as you. It may take time and work to find your support team—staying patient and knowing what you believe in will help.

In chapter 5, I am going to help you prepare for the insensitive things that people will say to you and how these statements can trigger your grief unexpectedly. I am also going to make you aware of these statements before they happen, so you can get yourself ready and not be totally thrown if you encounter them.

Chapter Four Contemplation Questions

1. Which of the eleven myths are you currently experiencing while coping with your cat's illness?

2. Now that you understand the myths surrounding pet loss grief, can you add some additional myths that you may have encountered? Can you debunk them and pull something positive out of them?

3. Take any of the eleven myths that you relate to and rewrite them to show the positive. Post them so that you can see them everyday.

5. Coping with the Triggers

When a co-worker, a stranger you meet at the grocery store, or even your best friend tries to reassure you by commenting, "It's only a cat . . . You can always get another!" new feelings and emotions may become activated, and your life in that moment changes. You start to feel uncomfortable, yet you don't know what to do. Should you just smile and say, "Thank you," or should you politely turn away and go about your business?

I am pleased we are having this conversation right now because I want to share with you—such comments are expected. It is common for people to say things that they think are helpful and well-meaning, but to you are very unsupportive and insensitive about your cat's illness and upcoming passing.

What is happening when people say these unintentionally unsupportive things is that they inadvertently fuel and activate your grief. You become sad, depressed, angry, or confused, and you are not sure why all of a sudden you are feeling this way. You likely become confused as to how to handle these people and even wonder if you should continue being friends.

Let me repeat—it is common for people to say unsupportive, yet what they think are well-meaning, things to someone who has a cat that is ill. And it is also normal for you to have the reactions that you are having.

Now here is the thing—as a society we have gotten very distant from the dying process. We view it as something to be afraid of, and we may even want to avoid death altogether. We have become afraid to talk about death openly and fear it is the end.

As people, the more we accept that death begins another cycle of life and the more we allow our grief to happen in a safe environment, then the healthier this natural process will be.

I am going to teach you how you can use what you've learned about grief itself (from chapter 1) and the stages of grief (from chapter 3), so you can handle unsupportive comments with compassion and grace. That's what we'll be addressing in this chapter.

Case Study — Joanne and Gogger

Joanne, whose Gogger had feline AIDS, told me in one of our Shoulder to Lean On sessions that after she'd told her best friend about Gogger, this person started to avoid her.

Joanne was confused and felt very alone. She explained, "My Gogger just got diagnosed with an advanced stage of feline AIDS, and I felt helpless and hopeless. All I wanted was my best friend, someone to talk to, but she is now avoiding me and my cat, and has said some really hurtful things. I heard she thinks she is going to catch AIDS from Gogger if she comes to visit me!"

You can expect this to happen to you. Because, as with Joanne's experience, people dread both illness and death, and some will avoid dealing with it—no matter what. As a society we aren't versed in how to go about supporting each other in a healthy way when someone is experiencing grief of any kind.

When Joanne became aware of the unsupportive things people were saying and prepared herself on how she was going to react, she found that her support team suddenly grew.

Your Preparation

Right now I want to share with you how you can be prepared for the hurtful things that people will say to you.

I promise you are going to hear them every day, not from everyone, but you will hear them from people that you thought understood what you are going through—just like what happened with Joanne.

This is a huge part of your journey when dealing with your cat's life-threatening illness. Be ready, be prepared, and take control of these situations, so you know what you are feeling is okay and customary.

Here are a few of the many things people typically say that my clients have experienced. (At the end of this chapter you will have the opportunity to list some of your own.)

Things That People Say—A List

1. It's only a cat . . . You can get another.

As a cat parent, you know that the relationship that you have with your cat is unique to the both of you. No one else has that exclusive relationship as you and your cat do. Cats are special individuals and when you have a strong bond, it is extremely special.

When someone says to you, "It's only a cat, and you can get another," this is the time for you to respond, "Thank you," and make your exit. To engage and try to educate this person only takes time away from your healing and your cat, which is the place to exert your emotional and physical energies during this special time.

The only thing that matters is that you realize how special your cat is to you—not the opinions of others.

2. I am so sorry to hear that.

This is a big one and the most popular thing to say when we get the news that someone's cat is sick. The fact is, it is not that person's fault that your cat is sick.

I know it may be a moot point, but a kinder, more supportive and compassionate way to respond to this type of news is "I am so sad to hear that your cat is sick." This type of comment will give you a safe place to express your grief rather than feeling like you have to take care of the other person's emotions.

The way you can react to this response is not to thank them. Because, remember, it is not your job to take care of someone else. Silence, a small smile, followed by a gentle head nod is all that is needed. If they persist, you can politely excuse yourself.

3. You are still grieving?

"You are still grieving?" is a very insensitive question to pose to someone that is feeling sad or depressed that their cat has a life-threatening illness. It suggests that there should be a time limit on the grief process and that you've taken it too far.

Prepare yourself by falling back on what you've learned about grief thus far in the book—grieving doesn't just go away, and it does not have a timetable. Remember, take as much time as is necessary with your grieving.

This question oftentimes helps people know who their real support team is. If you hear this, you can politely respond, "Yes, I am," and then make your exit. You really don't want to waste your time with people that just don't get it.

4. Let me tell you what I did for my cat . . .

This is another tough one. Although it may seem supportive, it can also be overwhelming and create feelings of guilt. You just got the news about your cat, and you are still trying to figure out how you are going to live your life with this new situation. Opening yourself up to a ton of advice at this time could be helpful, but it could also increase your feelings of anxiety, guilt, hopelessness, and being overwhelmed.

By making your personalized checklist (in chapter 2) and also designing daily and/or weekly plans with goals on how you are going to take care of your cat, you can then pick and choose what advice you want to listen to. We will explore this in more detail in chapter 8.

A good way to respond to this fourth comment is "I appreciate your thoughts of concern, but I really just need to just process my feelings at this time."

Please use the three *Contemplative Questions* at the end of this chapter to guide you to become aware of and prepare your responses to these kinds of statements.

Your Support Team

You are the expert when it comes to your grief journey and the caretaking of your cat. Your grief journey is unique, and no two people deal the same way with losing a cat to a life threatening-illness, such as cancer.

The important thing to remember is to choose wisely the people that you interact with during this special time. Choose those that truly support you, those that listen, don't judge you, and only give you advice when you ask them.

That type of support is available to you. You don't need to feel alone and go through this journey without support and compassion.

When you find these people, consider them friends to help you to not walk the journey of pet loss grief alone. In chapter 9, we will talk about ways in which you can get support.

Chapter Wrap-Up

This chapter aims to help you become aware of the unsupportive things that people are going to say to you while you are coping with your cat's illness. It is common—and it is also normal for their words to trigger grief in you. The key to responding to such statements with compassion and grace is to prepare yourself and to entrench yourself in the truth about grief and its seven stages. You will use this chapter's *Contemplative Questions* to help to become aware of and prepare your responses to these statements.

Also, you may want to actively find one, two, or more people who will serve as your "support team," listening to you and allowing you to live out your grief as it naturally happens.

In the next chapter, I am going share with you why it is important to celebrate the life you have with your cat, even though you are experiencing intense grief. I will share tips and actual routines that you can do. When you celebrate the life you have with your cat, it is another way that you are supporting yourself on your grief journey in a healthy way.

Chapter Five Contemplation Questions

1. Which of the "Things That People Say" have you experienced? Feel free to write down additional statements that you've heard and that have left you feeling more grief.

2. With each of the statements that you listed above, write down how you will respond to take control of the situation.

3. Can you list the ways in which you would like support with the pet grief that you are experiencing?

EXPERIENCING YOUR JOURNEY
SECTION TWO

Should you shield the valleys of the windstorms, you would never see the beauty of their canyons.

—Elisabeth Kubler-Ross

6. Celebrating Life

Taking Stock

Right now, I would like to ask you a few questions to help prepare you for the next part of your pet grief journey—living your journey.

- Are you feeling that the life of your cat is so incredibly special?

- Do you want to provide the best care you can for your cat?

- Do you now understand that your pet grief is natural and okay?

- Are you allowing your feelings of grief to happen without feeling like you are crazy?

- Are you ready to take some action on helping your cat through this special time?

- Are you also ready to take care of yourself?

If you answered *yes* to any of these questions, then that is wonderful because one of the most important things about healing your pet grief is to take stock on where you are in the process.

All the chapters in this section are about taking action for what you are going to do next for your cat and yourself. The journey is not about insulating yourself from feeling grief. In fact, nowhere in this book am I going to encourage you to stuff down your feelings or not honor where you are in your grief journey.

Why? It is not a healthy way to do grief. As I've already explained, staying present with your grief is necessary and extremely healthy. It takes work to actively manage grief.

By knowing how you are going to spend your time with your cat during this journey, you are setting yourself up to cope proactively and positively with the myriad feelings that will come up during this time.

Grief can be expected. Yet, the unexpected feelings that grief entails can rock your world if you are not prepared. And there are many more ways that I am going to continue to help you prepare in this book.

In previous chapters, you learned to recognize your emotions of grief on physical, emotional, and spiritual levels. Plus, you came to understand that your grief is unique to you, and it is natural.

Yet, there is so much more you can do for your healing to take place. For instance, in your pet grief journey, you will take the time to celebrate the life of your cat while they are still alive. This can only enrich and deepen your bond.

This chapter is about how you can celebrate the life of your cat while your cat is still alive. It's about creating new routines and spending time with your beloved companion in comfortable ways that focus around quality, not quantity, as the key.

You may ask—why is this important? This process is another step to help heal your pet grief journey. If your cat only lives for one week or is fortunate enough to live for ten more months, you can still do all the activities in this chapter. This chapter will provide the guidance for you to begin to create more inner peace.

So many of my clients report that incorporating these suggestions into their daily plans has made them strong, more decisive, and more grounded on their grief journeys. They've been able to make tough decisions and deal with veterinarians more thoughtfully (something we'll address more in chapter 12).

Case Study—Abigale and Moonlight

Abigale, who was working with me in my Shoulder to Lean On support program, found that when she began to celebrate the life she had with her cat, Moonlight, she felt more at ease with what she was going through. It helped her feel more in control during her pet grief journey.

By actively and thoughtfully determining how she would celebrate Moonlight's life, Abigale was actually able to do special things for Moonlight that made her feel really good.

One: How it worked is that Abigale first made a list of all the things she did for Moonlight in the same journal that you downloaded in chapter 2. For instance, Moonlight loved when Abigale brushed her nightly, fed her special treats, and played with the laser pointer.

As Abigale added to her list, she found that she remembered some things that she had long forgotten. Her list helped her realize how much she shared with Moonlight.

This simple task was healing and supported Abigale to recognize that her emotions of grief were to be expected since she shared a rich and rewarding life with Moonlight.

Yet, after the diagnosis, Abigale realized that Moonlight wasn't going to be able to endlessly chase after the laser pointer anymore or have the stamina to play hide-and-seek. She took into consideration the current state of Moonlight's health to figure out what Moonlight could do. For example, their nightly routine of bushing was perfect, and I even taught Abigale some basic massage and energy techniques that she could incorporate into her daily routine.

Two: At this point, Abigale then made a new list that included new ways to take care of Moonlight. Abigale found that by doing this, she came up with some new activities that helped her feel as if she had some control over what was happening to Moonlight. (In the next chapter, we will talk more about this in detail.)

Three: Abigale spent time researching. She made lists of options for additional care to help Moonlight feel more comfortable. This helped Abigale tremendously (we will cover this more in chapter 8).

The Importance of Celebrating

Let's face it—like Abigale, you got terrible news about your cat, and your life is completely changing. You are probably feeling a lot of stress right now. As you know from the opening section of the book, what you are experiencing is natural, common, and normal. Your grief is active as a result of the changes that have occurred and the tough decisions that you must make.

A healthy and edifying way to express your grief, as Abigale already demonstrated, is to celebrate the life that you and your cat had together. Make a list, write a story, and/or make a photo album that documents how you shared your life together. This exercise will allow you to fully embrace the relationship that you have with your cat in a very healing way.

Use the three *Contemplation Questions* at the end of this chapter to help you prepare for the "Celebrate the Life" part of your unique pet grief journey.

You can thank your cat or express that you are sorry for any moment in your past that you wish had been different: for example, not paying attention to your cat that one brief time when you were too busy. Again, as with the previous exercise, in doing this, you will allow yourself to fully embrace the relationship that you have with your cat in a very healing way by being present. Being present in your journey will help you create special moments in the remaining time that you have with your sweet buddy.

Provide your cat with comforting ways of assistance through this tough time in their life so that your furry companion can experience more comfort. Take care of yourself too so that you stay strong, healthy, and present to be there for your cat one hundred percent (more on this in chapter 9.)

The chapters in this second section, "Experiencing Your Journey," will offer you more examples and options about how you can celebrate your and your cat's life together. I'll be sharing tools that have helped so many of my clients, no matter how long their cats lived.

Please try to undertake as many of these suggestions as you can because you will be happy you did in the long run. I can promise you that your relationship with your special companion will deepen even more. The memories you create will live within your heart forever. Those memories will never go away.

By actually doing these activities, you will ease the potential stress and strain of the grief journey because you took the time to feel your grief. You created an action plan on how to live together with your cat during this special time before your cat dies.

Remember, this is an exceptional time for you and your cat. Cherish that and don't let anyone tell you that you are weird because you are caring for your pal in a very deep and loving way.

You are not weird. You are honoring and celebrating the life of your cat and your very special relationship together. Your cat gave you a ton of companionship and grounding, no matter what else was going on in your life.

Stay focused and give the love back to your cat the way you want. If there are people in your life who are judging you, that is okay. Don't pay attention to them. Politely excuse yourself and go on with your business that focuses around your cat. You will be so happy that you did so. Your life with your cat will be enriched beyond belief.

Trust in the process and celebrate the life that you have with your cat by implementing the tools as Abigale did for Moonlight. Invest in and cherish the journey for healing your pet grief.

Chapter Wrap-Up

In this chapter, I helped you become aware of why it is important to celebrate the life that you have right now with your cat, even though you are experiencing intense grief. You have the chapter's *Contemplation Questions* to help you prepare for the "Celebrate the Life" too.

You also learned that when you celebrate the life you have with your beloved companion, you are also offering yourself support on your grief journey in a healthy way.

In the following chapter, I will share in more detail why it is important to celebrate the life you have with your cat by creating new routines that are bonding for you and your cat. I will share tips on how these routines will create new memories that will help heal your pet grief.

Chapter Six Contemplation Questions

1. Now that you read this chapter and understand the importance of celebrating the life you have with your cat, identify the ways that you celebrate life with your cat. List the routines and activities that you and your cat have done together.

2. What are the favorite activities or routines that you can safely do together now?

3. What are some new or adapted activities or routines that you can create now for you and your cat that will make new memories?

7. Changing Routines

You are grieving so many losses in regard to your relationship with your cat. Not only is your cat ill, but also the things that they can do are changing. Even though your companion is still with you right now, your daily routines have and will continue to change.

We will concentrate on deeper and more comforting routines that you two can do together, which, of course, will depend on your cat's health level at this time. (Please note that in the next chapter, I will talk more about some special ways that you can care for your cat's health.)

Through these routines, you will create new memories for the times that you two share during this special period. And by creating new routines, you also give yourself the opportunity to reflect on and love your cat in different ways, which, in turn, helps your grieving process.

The Importance of Quality

Before we get into the how, what, and when of your revised routine plan, I would like to talk about quality. When healing your pet grief, a way to be truly effective and transformational is to spend the rest of your available time together very focused on your cat.

What this means is, for example, if you are relaxing on the couch, instead of reading your email on your device, take a deep breath, touch your cat, and send loving energy to them.

Honestly, after your cat has died, you will think back to all the quality moments when you gave your cat special attention. And feelings of guilt may not even exist. Why? Because you participated fully with your cat while they were still in your life, and you were not distracted.

The Comforting Routine List

The first thing that I ask my clients when we are working on this part of the healing pet grief journey is "What are the things that you like to do most with your cat, and what are the special things that your cat does that make you happy?" Basically, I have them write out lists.

Your list can be any number of things that you love to do with your cat and that your cat likes to do. Include everything, don't edit or wonder if your cat can still do them at this point. I included a list template in Your Cat Grief Support Kit that you downloaded at the beginning of this book. I also give you some examples in this chapter of some things you can include in this list.

The healing part of this exercise is that it gives you a chance to document and reminisce about your relationship. You will probably discover things that you forgot that you did together but really enjoyed. You will remember some of your cat's antics, personality traits, toys, routines, people, and other animals that were part of both of your lives.

I will warn you that reminiscing about your routines will bring up grief. Remember from previous chapters, especially the first and third, that it is okay and extremely healthy to feel pet grief.

Just keep in mind that what you are going through is normal and unique to your relationship with your cat. Going over these routines and antics will help you with many aspects of your grieving journey.

Here is an example of some of the things that Linda included on her Comforting Routine List. Linda's list was a lot longer than this, but I'm only including an excerpt. You will learn more about Linda and her cat, Ace, later in this chapter.

Comforting Routine List

Quiet times on the bed snuggling

Silly times with the laser pointer

Making Ace's special treats

Weekly brushing

Going to the pet store to buy new cat toy

Ace following me when I cleaned house

Listening to Ace meow at the window

Ace sleeping on my lap when I talked to clients

All our quiet times together

A Second List — Routines We Can Do List

Now, make a new list, the Routines We Can Do List, that includes the things that your cat can actually do now, even if your cat only has a very short time left. Include one or two things that you both enjoy and can do together. It might be as small as a scratch behind the ears. Know that that is okay. What you do with your cat is not about quantity at this stage; it is about the quality of the activity.

When making this second list, don't discard your first list, the Comforting Routine List. Instead, keep the first list in a special place to save for later memories. (We will cover this more in my fourth book in *The Pet Bereavement Series*.)

Be sure to include any activities from your Comforting Routine List that you and your cat can still do together on your new Routines We Can Do List (also in Your Cat Grief Support Kit). Begin to go through this new list, making notes on which ones are your favorites.

Here is an example of Linda's new list of Routines We Can Do—

Spend more quiet time on the porch

Give Ace daily energy treatments

Make Ace's special treats and feed him by hand

The Plan

Finally, make a plan. My clients find that the key to success when creating new adventures and for healing pet grief is to create daily and weekly schedules to do particular activities.

Depending on your schedule, you may only be able to allocate five minutes per day or up to five hours on certain days. For example, you could do something special like a five-minute body scratch during which you are totally focused on your cat. Or maybe you can massage your cat's neck and back. The point is to plan ahead and actively decide how much time and exactly when during each day that you will devote to being fully present to your cat.

You might be feeling that it is weird or unnecessary to schedule favorite activities. Please trust this process and understand why scheduling is important. With all the chaos that might be happening in your world right now, activities have a way of being forgotten. They get buried under the normal emotions associated with the grieving process—pain, stress, sadness, and confusion.

My clients who have taken the time to make activity plans found that they not only had more enriching and quality time with their cats, but their guilt was virtually non-existent after their cats died.

To understand how important these lists and the plan are in supporting you in your grief journey, please spend some time reflecting on the three *Contemplation Questions* at the end of this chapter.

Case Study — Linda and Ace

Linda and Ace, or Mr. Zen, had a wonderful relationship that I was honored to experience. When Linda received the news from her veterinarian about Ace's liver cancer, she called me immediately.

Even amidst this tragic news Linda developed a meaningful and touching Routines We Can Do List that she still cherishes even after Ace's death.

During Ace's short end-of-life journey, Linda wanted to be sure that she created quality experiences for him. He was very ill and did not have the energy to do many things that they had done before. Even still, Linda provided love, attention, and dedication to her companion.

Quickly she made her lists and came up with a daily plan. She mindfully set up times to engage with Ace and provide a deep heart connection with him. She cooked him special treats that he adored, and she lovingly fed him as they sat on the floor together. This simple yet powerful activity was crucial for Linda, and Ace found incredible joy with the quiet time he had with her.

Even though Ace, the Zen kitty, has died, Linda still works with me in my Rescue Joy from Pet Loss Grief support program. During a phone call, she told me that the lists and daily plans she'd created continued to help her tremendously even after Ace reached the end of his life.

She found that repeatedly reading her Routines We Can Do List supplied her with confidence and a firm sense of knowing that she had given her heart and soul to another living being that had given her so much in return. Linda's feeling of guilt was not very strong because she knew that she had done the best she could for Ace.

It may seem tedious or unnecessary to create these lists, but as you can see, they helped Linda better understand, process, and heal her grief. She eventually began to feel joy with the life that she had shared with Ace, and these lists helped her to do that.

Give yourself adequate time to do make your lists, just as Linda did. I promise the lists will be invaluable tools on your journey of healing pet loss grief.

Chapter Wrap-Up

In this chapter, I helped you become aware of all the routines and antics that you and your cat shared together by creating the Comforting Routine List. You then created a second list of new routines and memories that you can share together during this special time, the Routines We Can Do List. You made a schedule to ensure that you allocate time each day to doing these routines with your cat. Also, you know that the new activities can be very simple because the main point is quality, not quantity, and meeting your cat where they are actually at in terms of health.

Remember to visit the chapter's *Contemplation Questions* to understand how important these lists and the plan are in supporting you on your grief journey.

In chapter 8, I am going to share ways to help your pet feel more comfortable and hopefully suffer less anxiety during this time. You will also find out why it is important to include holistic healthcare in addition to regular medical care.

Chapter Seven Contemplation Questions

1. After creating your first list, the Comforting Routine List, that includes all the routines and antics that you and your cat have enjoyed, what feelings of grief are you experiencing?

2. After creating your second list, the Routines We Can Do List, which includes the activities that you and your cat can actually do now, what feelings of grief are you now experiencing?

3. When you create daily/weekly/monthly activity plans, how do your grief feelings change? How do your pet grief feelings change after you have done some of the planned activities?

8. Finding the Best Healthcare

Many of my clients search for multiple ways to take action to find the best healthcare possible for their terminally ill cats. It's important to them to get things into gear as soon as they can, so their cats can feel as comfortable as possible, given their cats' conditions. These clients want to be sure that they do the best they can for their cats and provide all possible quality healthcare.

Integrative healthcare for terminally ill animals is an area of great personal interest and experience to me. Aiding clients in finding the most supportive healthcare teams for their terminally ill cats is something I really enjoy and have vast experience doing. In fact, it is how my work as a massage therapist for humans, horses, and hounds developed into working with people and their terminally ill pets.

It is important when your cat is diagnosed with a life-threatening illness to get a good team of professionals on your side for your cat. When considering integrative veterinarian medicine, think about including a regular veterinarian and a holistic veterinarian, as well as other healthcare professionals.

One of the most important things to remember is to pick your team wisely. Be sure everyone is on your side and has your cat in their best interests. If someone on your professional team is not willing to respect your decisions and wishes, then it is time to find someone else who will.

Case Study — Donna and Snowflake

When Donna was ready to put Snowflake's healthcare team together, I coached her with this first task—finding a regular medical veterinarian that she trusted, that communicated well, and that respected her journey and choices.

Since Donna's current veterinarian didn't respect some of her holistic choices, she had to find a new veterinarian, but that was okay. It was the best for her and Snowflake during their journey.

Having a regular veterinarian and specialists on board can be useful when it comes to diagnosis, emergencies, and other tasks your holistic veterinarian may not include in their scope of practice.

Since Donna wanted to integrate holistic medicine into her cat's therapy, I guided her to do some research to locate a good holistic veterinarian. This took a little time, but within a week she found one that had experience. Plus, the person absolutely loved Snowflake.

The added bonus was that her new medical veterinarian was willing to communicate with her holistic veterinarian. This helped Donna because she didn't need to waste valuable time with an unsupportive team member. Both veterinarians were willing to work together, which gave Donna peace of mind.

A Healthcare Team — Medical and More

Having a healthcare team is a crucial first step to consider when you get the news that your cat is terminally ill.

Additionally, your healthcare team doesn't need to end with just the medical profession. There are many other types of holistic care professionals that you may want to consider adding to your team.

Massage Therapy

Having a trained feline massage therapist on your team can be helpful for a variety of reasons. If your cat tolerates touch massage, then it can help your cat relax and feel more comfortable if they are experiencing any pain. The pain may not be from the illness itself. The fact is, your cat might not be able to use their muscles like before, and the inactivity causes the muscles to become sore and stiff.

A gentle massage keeps the circulation moving. Massage can help with the removal of toxins in the bloodstream and allows for healthier muscle tissue. My cat clients love their massages.

You may find that your cat doesn't like touch. If that is the case, do not feel bad. There are many things that you can offer your cat that do not include touch.

Animal Reiki or Energy Practitioner

The other team member you might want to include is an animal Reiki practitioner or a practitioner that practices other forms of energy healing.

Reiki can balance your cat's energy to help them feel relaxed and calm, and to suffer less from anxiety during this time. When I work on my feline clients with Reiki or other forms of energy techniques, they begin to breathe more deeply, relax more, and settle into very calm states of mind.

There are many other forms of energy work that are extremely beneficial and that you may want to consider. Integrative Manual Therapy (IMT) and Tellington TTouch are two others that I incorporate into my practice with great results.

Acupressure or Acupuncture

Both of these modalities are extremely helpful and usually cats prefer this form of "touch." Acupuncture is when tiny needles are placed in strategic points to balance your pet's energy. Acupressure involves the same strategic points with a thumb applied, rather than a needle.

Both of these techniques have excellent results for a variety of issues. Relieving pain, increasing mobility, and lowering stress are just a few of the benefits that acupressure or acupuncture can provide.

Herbal Medicine

Herbal medicine is a great way to support a cat with a terminal illness. Herbs can help in supporting the immune system, pain relief, digestion, and more.

How to Choose

The three *Contemplative Questions* at the end of this chapter will help you choose the most appropriate and capable members of the healthcare team for your cat.

Please take the time to visit those questions and respond to them fully.

Without Delay

There are so many more options for you to consider when building your team. It can take some time and some patience, so I encourage all my clients, whether via in person, phone, or Skype consultations, to begin this process right away.

The important thing to remember when assembling your healthcare team is to choose a team that has the proper training, experience, and credentials.

For example, a human massage therapist not trained in feline anatomy could cause harm due to the fact the person does not know how the feline body functions. The same applies for energy work, acupuncture, Reiki, etc. Special training to apply these therapies to animals is necessary.

Case Study — Marilyn and Bolt

Marilyn rescued Bolt, a black tuxedo cat, in a high kill shelter. In fact, Bolt was slated for euthanasia in seven days because he was considered too old and had health issues.

Marilyn told me that when she walked past Bolt's cage, she noticed something about him that stirred a very deep feeling that she was unable to pass up.

Instead of a new kitty, Marilyn decided to adopt Bolt. She couldn't imagine such a sweet senior having his life ended. Even though Bolt had health issues, she wanted to be sure he had love and compassion during his last few months of life by providing him the best healthcare she could.

When he came home, Marilyn called me to guide her with learning effective touch therapies that would help Bolt feel more comfortable. I helped her not only put together a healthcare team but taught her how to administer a range of motion exercises, basic energy techniques, and how to energetically connect with Bolt.

When the time came that Bolt could no longer be comfortable in his physical body and euthanasia was imminent, Marilyn was able to be with him and provide him with much comfort.

With the energy techniques she learned from me and the acupressure points she learned from her veterinarian acupuncturist, she was able to manage Bolt's anxiety.

I was privileged to accompany Marilyn and Bolt on the day that he was being euthanized. The bond that Marilyn and Bolt shared was astonishingly profound. It was clear that Marilyn and Bolt shared a deep and unending love.

The Merit of Teamwork

Taking some time to get your team together can help you walk your journey of pet grief with a feeling of strength and purpose.

My clients often comment that after their cats have died, they feel so grateful they did this. They don't feel guilty about not doing enough for their cats. They did everything just right.

In fact, many were convinced that their cats got the best care possible because they had strong teams that consisted of a regular veterinarian, holistic veterinarian, feline massage therapist, and a person trained in energy work.

That feeling of accomplishment allowed them to not feel guilty. Feeling guilty after your cat dies, or even while your cat is alive, is a natural feeling of grief. Yet, it happens more when you don't go into action while your cat is still alive.

By understanding your grief (chapters 1, 3, and 4), choosing carefully your friends that are going to support you (chapter 5), spending quality time with your cat while they are still alive (chapter 7), and picking a support team based on the needs of your pet, you will feel like you did all that you could. You will be offering your beloved cat the utmost support, and you will be offering yourself the same.

The clients who choose to find the best teams possible are the ones that say, "I gave my cat the best care I could, and I feel really good about that."

Chapter Wrap-Up

Finding the proper healthcare for your cat is critical to the process of not only helping your cat feel better but also helping you with your grief process. Your healthcare team will be composed of not only the veterinarian but also holistic animal healthcare practitioners.

Choosing practitioners who respect you, your cat, and your choices is essential. Take the time to research, interview, and get referrals for the practitioners that you choose to be on your team. Use the chapter's *Contemplative Questions* to assist you too. This careful consideration and building of the healthcare team will help both your cat in their last days, months, and years, and you on your grief journey.

In the next chapter, I am going to share with you tips on how to take care of yourself—in areas that do not include your cat.

I am going to give you reasons and examples of ways in which you can restore yourself during this special time. Plus, you will learn that it is okay to want take some alone time away from your cat.

Chapter Eight Contemplation Questions

1. What are some holistic modalities that you would like
    to include for helping your cat? Massage? Energy
    work? Acupuncture? Something else?

2. Do you feel comfortable asking your regular medical
    veterinarian if they would be on your team if you
    wanted to include a holistic veterinarian? What makes
    you comfortable or uncomfortable about asking?
    What can you do to feel more comfortable asking this
    question?

3. Make a list of the questions that you would ask each
    member of your team. They may include:

    a. Do you support holistic veterinarian medicine?

b. Are you willing to communicate with other members of the healthcare team?

c. What is your training in?

d. How much experience do you have?

e. Are you credentialed and/or licensed?

f. Do you have any clients whom I can talk to about the work you do?

9. Caring for Yourself

When you get the news that your cat is going to die, your first response may very well be that you want to spend 24/7 with them because you just don't know how much time you may have left together. This is a normal and very natural response.

However, allowing time in your schedule for self-care that does not involve your cat will actually make the time you do spend together with your cat higher in quality.

While all of my clients feel the guiltiest about taking time away from their cats to care for themselves, everyone needs to know that it is totally okay to do this. Not only is it okay, it is necessary. Self-care is actually a great way to manage your pet grief to allow greater focus, strength, and compassion to shine through.

Case Study — Rachael and Avalanche

As soon as Rachael heard from her vet that Avalanche had cancer, she literally stopped her life and devoted all her time to him. She stopped calling her friends, she didn't leave the house, and she slept on the floor to be closer to Avalanche. When she called me, she was exhausted because her anxiety was keeping her up all night.

What happened? Rachael stopped taking care of herself. She felt that she had to be with Avalanche and could never leave his side.

Although this is a wonderful story of devotion, Rachael was finding that she didn't even have the energy to continue at the pace of care she was giving Avalanche.

When she told me this, we immediately set up a self-care plan that was a balance of care for Avalanche and for her. With this plan she was able to experience some substantial positive changes. Her anxiety was less intense, and she was able to give the love that she wanted to Avalanche in his last weeks. Plus, when faced with some challenging decisions, she felt as if she could truly process the given information to make the best choice possible.

The Best Advice

Now please listen closely to the best advice that I can give you right now and that I gave to Rachael—carve out time to replenish your own body, mind, and soul. It's necessary and important.

You can give your cat a ton of attention during this special time. However, if you are tired, burned-out, stressed-out, not eating, and not sleeping because you feel the need to be with your beloved companion 24/7, then the quality of that time will suffer and important decisions will be difficult to make.

This is the time to take care of yourself so that you are functioning as best you can and not relying on your reserve.

As Rachael discovered, having strength is critical to be ready for the unexpected feelings of grief, the emergencies, and the challenging medical decisions you must make.

The "What" of Self-Care

There are many things that you can do for yourself that don't cost a lot of money, like walking in nature, taking a nap, taking a bath, hanging out with friends, listening to relaxing music, or having a cup of tea.

The important thing is to create a self-care plan that you know you can do. It's not important how many things you have on your list. The important thing is to create success for yourself. Include new activities that you would love to experience and old activities that have already given you joy and grounding.

In previous chapters and even in the next chapters, we will continue to explore more ways of honoring your cat, but for now just focus on yourself.

Remember, the healthier you are in body, mind, and spirit, the easier it is to cope and deal with the grief that you are going through and to be present for your cat in their final period of life.

The Physical Self

Let's talk about some of the options for taking care of your physical body during this time. These activities that you will do for yourself are not in combination with the activities that you are doing with your cat right now because this is about time for you!

My clients find that when they do one or more of the following physical things for their bodies, they feel stronger and more in control of their grief. Even if they can do something for only five to ten minutes a day, it still helps them on their journeys.

I will suggest that you spend at least a half-hour every day, if you can, with any combination of the following activities for the health of your body.

- Get a massage.

- Walk in nature.

- Undergo Reiki or another form of energy bodywork.

- Participate in an exercise class.

- Eat well and throughout the day.

- Get your sleep.

- Take short breaks throughout the day with your eyes closed.

- Breathe intentionally and actively.

If a half-hour every day is too much time, try to give yourself a half-hour at least three times a week to take care of your physical body.

The Mental Self

The next thing to take care of is your mind. As you know, your mind is going in a million different directions right now. Sometimes your mind clutter is creating so much anxiety and stress, you wonder how you are going to get through this.

To help your mind, you can find support groups, pet loss grief coaches, psychotherapists, friends, co-workers, family members, and veterinarians who totally respect the journey of pet grief that you are going through. They should be there for you and be able to walk this journey with you so that you don't have to feel alone.

Finding ways to support your mind's health can take some time, but if you know what you are looking for, the process can be less stressful.

Here are some of the ways that you can create a healthy mind that can support you.

- Talk to a pet grief coach—a coach will listen and guide you so that you can better manage your healing process.

- Talk to a psychotherapist or other healthcare provider—it is important to find someone that gets pet loss.

- Pet loss support groups—these provide another way to support you. In them you will meet people who are going through similar situations. Be sure you find one where you feel that you are getting ample time to express your journey and are not being judged by anyone.

- Friends and family—this is a tough one. Your friends and family may mean well, yet they may also be the ones who trigger your grief because they really don't know how to support you. Choose wisely and choose only those friends and family who let you talk and who don't offer advice. Definitely stay away from the ones who judge you!

A healthy mind is a strong mind that creates balance when mind clutter starts getting out of hand. Having a support system helps you monitor your mind and offers solutions when your grief is swirling out of control.

Choose a couple of these options that feel good to you. Do some research and don't feel bad if the person you thought was your best friend doesn't support you. There is someone who will!

The Spiritual Self

Now let's talk about your spiritual health. Many times you can forget about this one when experiencing pet grief. You may even be uncomfortable with your spiritual beliefs or may not have any.

Whatever your spiritual choice, remember it is your journey. I encourage you to only incorporate a spiritual practice into your daily life if you feel comfortable.

Here are some of the ways that you can create spiritual health in your life.

- Meditation comes in all forms. A quiet walk in the woods is equally meditative as sitting quietly in one posture and clearing your mind of all thoughts.

- Yoga, tai chi, and other forms of spiritual physical practice help your body become stronger. The discipline and focus create a connection to your inner spiritual force.

- Practicing your spiritual belief, no matter what your belief is, daily, weekly, or periodically, can help you receive solace.

- An animal communicator is a great way to get peace of mind and learn the spiritual connection that you have with your cat from your cat's perspective.

I have shared with you many ways to take care of yourself. It is totally up to you on how you would like to include one or many of the suggestions that I offered.

Remember, this is a trying time for you. You are getting bombarded with so much information, and the stress may be wearing you down.

Creating a support team for yourself is equally important as creating a support team for your cat (from chapter 8). Taking care of yourself is important because you want to have the physical energy and presence of mind to provide the best you can for your cat. It is difficult to do that if you are tired, hungry, stressed-out, suffering from body aches, and more.

Use the three *Contemplation Questions* at the end of the chapter to take action on your own self-care without guilt. Even if the only thing you can do right now is simple breathing to create balance in your life, that is okay!

Chapter Wrap-Up

In this chapter, I shared ways that helped so many of my clients find peace of mind and strength. I encouraged you to take some time for yourself without feeling guilty. Care for yourself in terms of your body, mind, and spirit.

By allowing time in your schedule for self-care, you will be able to spend more quality time with your cat. You'll make better decisions and be ready for unexpected grief too, just as was true for my client Rachael.

Remember to use the three *Contemplation Questions* to determine the what, when, and how of your own self-care.

In the next chapter, I am going to offer support for when you have the feeling that you just can't do enough for your cat. You will learn how to deal with the overwhelming feelings of guilt and anger, as well as other forms of pet grief, when you feel like you just haven't done enough. Plus, it is a sure-fire way to let your cat know that you love them.

Chapter Nine Contemplation Questions

1. What are one or two activities that you can do to take care of your physical body this week?

2. What are one or two ways that you can reach out to get support for the health of your feelings and thoughts (mind)?

3. If you are a spiritual person and have gotten away from your practice, how can you begin incorporating your beliefs into your everyday life?

10. Saying Thank You

If you are feeling unsure of what else you can do for your cat or if you are feeling stuck and even suffering with guilt that you are not doing enough for your cat, I would like to assure you that your feelings are universal and normal. You are not alone, and these feelings are part of the pet grief journey. In fact, you are exactly in the right place with your pet grief.

When my clients reach this point of feeling overwhelmed, I suggest that they begin telling their cats, "Thank you for everything that you gave me in life."

As a passionate cat-lover, you probably do this already. Yet, there are ways to talk with your beloved companion that can create a sense of being listened to and understood. That's what I want to teach you to do.

It really isn't that hard, and I teach people all over the world to do it.

What to Do + A Case Study — Norma and Babette

This is a special time for you and your cat. Creating a comfortable, peaceful, and healing journey for the both of you is one of the most important things to consider.

It is important to ask yourself, "How am I going to strengthen my relationship with my cat so that when the end of their life is imminent, I am able to participate fully? How am I going to give everything I can to my cat as they reach the end of life?"

First Step: Let's begin by setting some intentions or goals on what you would like to tell your cat. I am going to share with you how Norma planned to begin talking with her cat, Babette.

Norma and I had a few conversations in my Shoulder to Lean On program because she wanted to be sure that she was thorough. She didn't want to leave anything out of the conversation.

I am going to share with you five of the most critical things on Norma's list and that most of my clients want to have answered.

1. How am I going to say thank you to Babette while she is still alive?

2. What are the ways that I am going to tell her that I am sorry?

3. How am I going to tell Babette that I love her?

4. What did Babette teach me?

5. How am I going to tell Babette that I will be okay when she dies and to not worry about me?

Please feel free to use these for your own planning. Also, use the *Contemplation Questions* at the end of the chapter and Your Cat Grief Support Kit that you downloaded at the beginning of this book when creating the message that you want to tell your cat.

After Norma recorded her answers on paper, she read it all out loud a few times to herself. She experienced grief yet channeled her feelings of grief to answer her questions.

You can do this as well. After you choose any of questions above or even some of your own, write them down. Say them out loud a few times. Allow your feelings of grief to happen. And at the same time, use these strong feelings to guide you in finding the most complete answers to the questions.

Remember, your feelings and emotions are normal, and it is very important to let them out rather than stuff them in.

One of the biggest regrets that I hear from people who come to me after their cats have died is that they wish they'd told their cat how much they loved them. They wish they'd thanked them for sharing life with them. Many even are painfully sorry that they didn't pick their cats up in their arms when their cats were rubbing across their legs.

If you do this activity now, you will feel better about your journey in the future. Norma was so happy that she spent the time doing this for Babette.

Step Two: Decide when and where you will have the conversation.

You now have a list of what you would like to share and tell your cat. Are you wondering how to do it? Are you wondering if your cat is going to understand you?

Rest assured that your cat does understand you. Your cat is an expert in reading your body language, hearing your voice, and understanding you better than anyone. No need to worry that they won't understand or hear you.

Instead, your job is to create a special time so that you can respectfully talk to your cat. This is not to say that you can't talk to your cat while carrying out household chores, snuggling on the couch, or while your cat walks across your keyboard. Any type of communication is fine whenever the mood strikes you.

For deeper healing purposes, it is important to take time out from your busy day to create calm. Be totally focused on sharing the things that you want to share with your cat.

I would recommend going to a place with your cat where you will not be disturbed. This place may be a quiet room in your home or under a tree. Try and keep the activity relaxed so that the both of you can make a heart connection.

Norma and Babette sat in a sunny window one afternoon. Norma told Babette how much she loved her while Babette purred in the sunlight.

The beauty of this is that you are setting the stage for some deep, meaningful communication. You are also actively healing your pet grief. Plus, you are sharing a time together that is calm, intentional, and peaceful as we discussed earlier in chapter 7.

Step Three: Once you have chosen the place where you would like to talk with your cat and you know that you will not be disturbed, look into the eyes of your cat and smile. It is okay to touch and pet your cat if they find enjoyment with this activity.

Then close your eyes and take a few deep breaths. Settle the chaos in your mind and relax. I have a great meditation for you to download on my website (you can find the link for this gift in the Resources section of this book) that will help you with this. Once you are calm and ready, begin to talk to your cat.

If you choose to tell your cat that you love them, also explain all the things that you love about them. Talk to your cat as you would another adult. Try not to baby talk as it dilutes the power of your intention.

The important thing is you are talking to your cat and making a conscious effort to tell them everything that they mean to you.

Something else to consider is that you can do this more than one time. You can have this same talk with your cat as many times as you like. For example, Norma had conversations like this with Babette every morning after breakfast.

Extreme Healing

This exercise is extremely healing. Even still, as you talk to your cat, your grief feelings will probably begin to come alive again.

Remember, grief is natural, common, and normal, and it is part of life. Allow your feelings of grief to come out. Tell your cat what you are feeling. Your cat is your best friend, and even though they are ill, your cat still wants connection with you.

So much healing can take place with this activity. And my clients are so thankful when they reflect back to this time. They often comment on how glad they are that they took this opportunity to talk to their cats.

Norma was so happy that she got a chance to tell Babette that she was sorry and that she loved her.

The Difficult One

One of the biggest successes is from those clients that told their cats, "I will be okay, and it is okay to die."

This is a difficult one. Because, really, are you going to be okay after your cat dies?

If you find this task difficult, please take your time to process your feelings of grief. It isn't necessary to rush or push yourself because this could be the most challenging thing to say to your cat and you want to be sure you mean it.

One way that I help my clients is to ask them to listen to what their hearts are telling them. Then reflect on all the things their cats provided that they are thankful for. I can promise there will be a tiny hidden place where you will know you will be okay after your cat dies.

By telling your cat it is okay to die when they are ready, I can assure you that your heart will open to receive amazing and healing insights on this part of your journey.

Chapter Wrap-Up

It is normal to experience overwhelming feelings that you are not doing enough for your cat. Know that these are normal, and also take action. By talking to your cat in a well-planned way, you will be able to cope with those extreme pet grief feelings.

Remember how healing and powerful this talking experience was for Norma and Babette.

Use the three *Contemplation Questions* to help you design, plan, and implement your special conversation with your cat. You can also use Your Cat Grief Support Kit that you downloaded.

In the next chapter, we will address the tough decisions you'll likely encounter as your cat reaches the end of life. You will begin to learn how to be prepared for this very difficult time.

Chapter Ten Contemplation Questions

1. Now that you read about Norma and Babette, what do you want to tell your cat? List everything that you want to say to your cat.

2. As you make your list, what are the feelings of grief coming up for you?

3. Where is the special place that you are going to tell your cat the things that you want to say? How are you going to tell your cat?

REMAKING YOUR JOURNEY
SECTION THREE

Grief is in two parts. The first is loss.
The second is the remaking of life.

—Anne Roiphe

11. Preparing for the Last Day

Probably the last thing that you want to think about right now is how you are going to prepare for the last day of your cat's life.

Maybe you are asking yourself, "Isn't it enough to feel and get in touch with my grief? Won't being in touch with my grief help me during the last few days, hours, moments, and even after my cat dies?"

Yes, it will! It is very important to know and understand everything that you are going through to heal your pet loss. Yet, I can promise you that if you spend some additional time preparing for your cat's last day, you will have a different, more manageable experience.

This experience will leave you knowing that you did the best you could for your cat. Therefore, you may experience less chaos because you know you were prepared for this day.

In this section, I am going to support you with making some rough decisions about dealing with this part of your grief journey. I am going to share some amazing tools that my clients have used over and over again to help guide them through this extremely tough time.

Quick Recap

You have come a long way and have created some beautiful moments with your cat. These incredible memories will bring many moments of joy to your soul.

Understanding that grief is not only normal but also that how you experience it is unique is imperative. It is vital to the relationship that you have with your cat right now.

You also know that it is healthy to experience grief and it is something you cannot avoid. To express your pet grief in the various ways talked about in this book, you will walk the grief journey with incredible personal empowerment. Plus, you may even find some joy in your process, which we will talk about in chapter 15.

Let's begin to explore how you can do this by preparing for the last day of your cat's life.

The Stages of Final Day Preparation

As with the rest of the grief process, preparation for the last day of your cat's life comes in stages. I am going to help you be prepared for these stages in the next few chapters.

Chapter 12—Preparing your plan ahead of time will help you make some really hard decisions. One of the biggest and most avoided considerations that my clients face as they spend the last few days, weeks, or months with their cat is "When is the right time to euthanize my cat?"

If you are stressing over this decision, know that you are not alone. All of my clients stress over this question each time their cats are approaching the end of their lives.

The final act from this decision is permanent, and for all good reasons you want to make sure your timing is perfect. We will talk about this more in chapter 12. I will support you with ways to help you prepare, so you can make this difficult decision with less stress and anxiety.

Chapter 13—We are going to spend time writing a love letter to your cat. This letter will be a proclamation of appreciation, healing, and apology (if needed). It will also include anything else that you might want to express to your cat at the time of death.

I will share with you the importance of writing something down and then reading it to your cat at the time of death to increase your heart connection. It will also help you with any lingering pet loss grief feelings of guilt, denial, and anxiety.

Chapter 14—It is also important for you to know what you can expect after your cat reaches the end of life. I am going to help you be prepared for your grief through the death experience in chapter 14. It is somewhat similar to what you have been coping with currently with your cat. Yet, there are some very important changes to be aware of for your healing. For example, people around you are going to react differently, and your expectations for your own behavior are going to increase.

I am going to guide you to be prepared for this time when your soul feels empty and loneliness settles in.

Chapter 15—Finally, I offer supportive tools that will guide you on what you can do next. Expectations are still going to increase from the people around you. Perhaps, you will be placing heavy expectations on yourself too.

This period does take time to adjust to, and we will talk about ways that you can move through it with grace and compassion for yourself.

To begin preparing for your cat's final day, please take time to respond to the three *Contemplation Questions* at the end of the chapter.

Case Study — Kim and Bitsy

The pet loss grief journey is one of the most profound experiences that you can have. Sharing life with a cat can offer many unique and heart-warming life lessons even with the most independent cat.

I am sure you have people in your life who love you tremendously and whom you love. But do you really have anyone in your life that loves you unconditionally, without judgment?

So many people believe cats are incapable of giving unconditional love without judgment, but for Kim, her experience with Bitsy was filled with love and nonjudgment.

Kim had a great support system of friends, co-workers, and some family members. Kim is the type of person that everyone loves. Yet, she told me that even though they all loved her and gave her a ton of support, they still judged her when she was still grieving the fact that Bitsy was dying.

Kim told me, "Bitsy is the love of my life. She has been with me for 14 years, going through the ups and downs of life with me. She is my constant companion and follows me through the house. She taught me about love when I didn't love myself. In fact, she is still teaching me about love. She doesn't care how I look or how I act—Bitsy is always ready to curl up in my lap, no matter how I am feeling."

Kim learned that the lessons Bitsy showed her were some of the greatest gifts that she could ever receive. Kim experienced life-changing moments through Bitsy's patience and nonjudging love. She learned that she did not need to criticize herself even though others did.

The unconditional love that Bitsy gave to Kim provided Kim with the self-assurance to know that she was a really great person.

The Goal of Preparation

Another point that I would love for you to consider is that your feelings of personal grief will be incredibly strong when the last day of your cat's life comes.

My goal is to help you be prepared when this last day arrives, so those decisions do not have to be made at the last minute. You already know what you are going to do. You have a plan that you feel good about. In this way, there will be less chaos at this difficult moment in your life.

The goal is that when this day comes, you can look into your cat's eyes and know that it is time. Your plan becomes your self-support tool that will help you stay clear and present. You will be able to be completely attentive to the needs of your cat, rather than making last-minute decisions. You don't want to lose out on a very special moment in your journey with your cat.

When your cat reaches the end of life, this is the time that you do not want to be scrambling. It is a time for you to be there for your cat when they may be going through fear and anxiety.

This is a special time because the more you can be attentive to your cat's needs, the better you will feel after your cat is no longer in your life.

Chapter Wrap-Up

You've begun to realize how important it is to have a plan of action so that you can be prepared for the myriad decisions that you will have to make on the final day of your cat's life.

You also learned that your cat taught you about unconditional love without judgment and how that can make you a better person. Kim and Bitsy's story exemplified this powerful relationship.

Use the three *Contemplation Questions* to begin to prepare for your cat's last day.

In the next chapter, you will learn how to make some tough decisions for your cat. This will help you feel more control during a very chaotic time. The next chapter will guide you through the process of preparation for the last day so that you feel grounded and ready for this extremely tough time.

Chapter Eleven Contemplation Questions

1. Now that you read about Kim and Bitsy, determine how your cat supports you with unconditional love.

2. As you list these ways of support from your cat, what feelings of grief come up for you? How do you feel about these feelings?

3. What are some of the ways that you have become a better person because of your cat?

12. Surviving the Tough Decisions

One of the biggest decisions and the most anxiety-producing question that I get from my clients is "When do I know the time is right to euthanize my cat?"

This decision is by far a very difficult one, and, as decisions go, no one really wants to make this one at the wrong time. And this decision is a crucial one.

When you determine early in your pet loss journey how you are going to deal with euthanasia, it can help you stay focused on your cat when they need you the most. This time can be extremely chaotic, and the last thing you want to be doing is making a last-minute decision that had no thought behind it.

The Two Big Questions

When Carrie was ready to talk to me about making this decision for her cat, Rosebud, she had two main questions. These same two questions are the ones that most of my clients have asked me.

You may be asking yourself these questions as well . . .

1. How do I know when the right time is?

2. When is the best time to euthanize my cat?

Although these questions are tough, they are very important. And by answering them in your unique way, it will help you with many of the grief stages and emotions that you are going through.

Question One

Let's start with the first one, "How do I know when the right time is?" It's a hard question. At first, no one can really answer it without doubt and without questioning if their answer is correct.

Yet, based on Carrie's experience with Rosebud, my own experiences with my own pet loss, and the experiences of many of my clients, I can tell you that when you are clear with your answer, it can help you feel incredibly connected to your cat.

Knowing the answer to this question and not doubting your decision will also help with some of the most prevalent feelings of grief, such as guilt, anxiety, anger, and depression.

When is the right time?

First—ask for your veterinarian's opinion. If you have more than one veterinarian, ask each and every one of them. They deal with pet loss almost every day. Their experienced answers can guide you with the first stage of answering this question for you and your cat.

They will probably give you the following answers. I encourage you to explore your feelings with each of these options.

The time is right . . .

- when the quality of life of your cat is no longer the way it was.

- when your cat is in a lot of pain.

- when your cat can't walk.

- when your cat is unable to respond.

- when your cat's bodily functions are no longer functioning or not under your cat's control.

- when your cat loses their dignity.

- when your cat tells you.

All of these answers are useful and extremely important for you to consider. However, they do not take into consideration your process and the unique relationship that you have with your cat. This is important for you to consider before your cat is approaching the end of life.

Second—if you have a great support team, ask them. They can offer you a lot of support.

It isn't worth it if you ask people who don't understand what you are going through. This lack of support will only create more stress and anxiety around your decision-making.

Third—if you are working with a pet loss grief coach, be sure to spend time exploring this topic. Your coach will help you set up a unique plan that will support you with making the best decision around this topic, as well as other topics, in a meaningful way.

Something to keep in mind if you are asking the opinion of others: even though their opinions are important, remember, you are the one who lives with and cares for your cat every single day. Along with their opinions, you and your cat will know best.

Many of my clients are thankful for this exercise early in their pet loss journeys even though it is a difficult decision to contemplate.

Please note—if your grief feelings are affecting you so much that you have suicidal thoughts or you are unable to function, seeing a psychotherapist or medical practitioner is a necessary choice for you at this time.

Question Two

When is the right time to euthanize my cat?

You have collected the opinions of your veterinarians, and you know your cat better than anyone. You know when your cat is uncomfortable or is resting quietly. You know when your cat is happy or sad. You know when your cat is in pain and struggling through life.

You can just look into your cat's eyes or watch their body language and know what your cat is saying to you. Right?

Once you have your veterinarian's opinion and worked on your own feelings about the end-of-life process, it is now time to ask your cat.

Asking Rosebud

During one of our calls, Carrie fretfully asked me, "How will I know when the time has come to make this decision? I don't want to mess up."

I guided her with the answer, "Rosebud will tell you."

Carrie told me later that this was the best advice she could have ever gotten from anyone. It was pivotal in calming her anxiety that had been developing into panic due to her feelings of uncertainty.

Carrie continued to share that one morning when they both woke up, she had a nagging feeling that something was changing. When she looked over at Rosebud, she could see that Rosebud was different somehow. The brightness was no longer there. Because Carrie already had planned for this and knew Rosebud would give her the answer, she asked, "Rosebud, are you ready?" Carrie shared that she got an overpowering sense that, yes, Rosebud was ready. When Carrie asked, Rosebud picked up her head and looked deep into Carrie's eyes in an entirely different way than what she was accustomed to.

I am not saying here that this was easy for Carrie. Yet, she didn't question herself because she was prepared. Instead, she trusted the relationship that she had with Rosebud and what she had discerned.

You know the relationship that I am talking about. It is the same one that you have with your cat that is based on trust and mutual respect.

The Human-Animal Bond

We are their caretakers from the moment they set their paws in our homes. They are our family. The human-animal bond is different than what we have with our friends and other family members.

Your cat trusts you to make the best decisions for them that are based on the life that you spent together—even if they don't act like they do. When the time comes, be prepared for your cat. On a spiritual level they appreciate it.

Don't wait until your cat has reached the end of life to make these decisions. Take the time now to determine the answers to these questions, even though it is extremely hard and may bring up more feelings of grief that you would like to avoid. You will be doing your cat a service and giving them the best care by preparing ahead of time for their final day.

Work with the three *Contemplation Questions* at the end of this chapter to receive further guidance in this process so that you know that you made the right decision at the right time.

Carrie has been extremely thankful and happy she answered these questions early on. By doing so, she felt extremely prepared and present for Rosebud when the time came. She had a lot less guilt and panic. She didn't have to scramble during a potentially chaotic time.

Instead, she was able to give Rosebud her full attention during the euthanasia, holding her and soothing her throughout the entire process.

Chapter Wrap-Up

In this chapter, we talked about ways in which you can get support for making one of the toughest decisions you will ever have to make for your cat. Although it may be painful, it will be beneficial to you and your cat to work out your answers to these two tough questions early on.

I shared with you seven tips that can help you to make this decision in a very meaningful way. Use this advice to guide you during this very difficult time. Also, use the three *Contemplation Questions* to help ensure that you make the right decision at the right time.

In chapter 13, I am going to show you how you can proclaim in a very special way your appreciation, love, and respect for your cat. This tool will give you a way to heal any regrets that you may have for not giving your furry companion more time or energy.

Chapter Twelve Contemplation Questions

1. What are your feelings about each of the seven tips that I shared about making a decision about euthanasia?

2. What feelings of pet grief come up for you when you reflect on these tips?

3. What tips are you going to pay most attention to during this special time that you have with your cat?

13. Writing a Love Letter

If you are at the point in your journey where you want to do something very special for your cat that will last forever, that's wonderful.

Maybe you would like to create a very different way to tell your cat how much you love them. However, your mind clutter may be a little chaotic with all your thoughts and feelings at this point. Remember, that is okay.

It doesn't matter where you are in your journey because writing a love letter to your cat at any time is a wonderful way to heal your pet grief.

When you can collect and express the love that you have for your cat in a love letter, it is extremely helpful for your pet grief journey.

Are you not sure where to begin?

That is okay. I am going to help you and encourage you to spend some time every day jotting down special memories or things that you want to tell your cat.

Even spending only five to ten minutes a day writing down some special remembrances will help you. It will lead to your writing a personal and meaningful love letter to your cat.

Keep in mind that this is your proclamation of appreciation, healing, apology (if needed), and inclusion of anything else that you may want to express to your cat before the time of death.

Yet, if there is not time for you to do this before your cat reaches the end of their life, that is okay too. It is still an incredibly healing process to do even after your beloved companion dies.

My clients who work with me in my Rescue Joy from Pet Loss Grief program have found healing and solace, no matter when they wrote their love letters. In my course, clients write a series of letters that help them move through coping with pet loss with grace, respect, and compassion for themselves.

Case Study — Justine and Pine

You may be asking, "Why should I write things down and read it to my cat?" That is a common question. Often writing is not a favorite activity—until you write your first letter.

Justine found this when she wrote her letter to her cat, Pine. She discovered how important it was to put her thoughts and feelings down on paper.

She hated to write, but when she started to jot down special memories that she shared with Pine, she changed her mind.

After she collected all her thoughts, she wrote her love letter to Pine. She read it to him out loud and later told me, "I just loved the process of writing a love letter. I didn't think I would, but after I started jotting memories down, I found I couldn't stop. It was so healing for me. Then when I read my love letter to Pine, I was convinced he understood what I was telling him. It increased our bond during a very difficult time. I am so glad I did this."

Justine experienced this exercise as a declaration of love to her cat. Writing a love letter and then reading it out loud helped her with any lingering feelings of pet grief, such as guilt, denial, and anxiety, that she had been experiencing.

Step 1 — Essential Questions

Here are some questions that I share with my clients who are working through the Rescue Joy from Pet Loss Grief program. Each week there are about ten to twelve questions that encourage and support them through this tough time.

These questions will also help you pinpoint the feelings of compassion and love that you have for your cat.

Before you answer these questions, have a designated place where you will write your answers. It may be a special journal, your computer, or just a piece of paper. Also, remember to use the information that you wrote down in Your Cat Grief Support Kit that you downloaded at the beginning of this book.

Be sure to keep all of your answers in one place so that when you are ready to write your love letter, you have everything in front of you.

1. What did it feel like when you first met your cat?

2. How did you choose to bring your cat home?

3. What were the things that you loved to do for your cat as the caretaker?

4. What are you sorry for, and how can you apologize to your cat?

There is no need to answer these questions all at once unless you are really motivated to do so. When you answer these questions, keep in mind that no one is going to read them except you. Write down whatever comes to your mind without judgment and editing.

The important thing is to get your feelings out on paper so that you are ready to write your love letter.

After you answer all the questions above and maybe some of your own, let your journal sit for a couple of days. You may find you forgot something and want to add to it. A memory of you and your cat contemplating the birds at the feeder, strategizing the best laser playtime, or your cat sleeping all cuddled up on your computer desk might come back to you.

Keep in mind though that this letter doesn't have to be perfect. Your cat doesn't mind that you spelled something wrong or that your sentence isn't complete. Your cat is just happy to know that you are with them on this journey because it can be stressful for them as well, even for the most independent of cats. When our beloved companions are ill, they need us to provide comfort and safety.

The more that you can give back to your cat at their end-of-life period, the better you are going to feel after your cat has died. Even if you only have a week after the diagnosis to deal with your grief, whatever you can do will help you.

At the same time, please keep in mind that this exercise is not time-sensitive. If you are a person who only has moments left before your cat dies, writing a love letter after they die is extremely helpful for processing your grief.

Step 2 — The Love Letter

After you feel like you have everything down that you want to tell your cat, it is now time to take out a fresh piece of paper or open a new Word document and write your love letter.

The first thing to do is put the date on the top of your letter. The reason for this is that sometime in the future, whether months or years from now, you will probably come across your letter. It will help you put in perspective where you were in coping with your pet loss journey and how far you have come.

You might even want this letter as a eulogy for your cat's funeral if you choose to mourn your loss in this manner. We will cover pet funerals in detail in the fourth book of *The Pet Bereavement Series: My Cat Has Died: What Do I Do?*

Then start your letter with "Dear [name of your cat]." I suggest beginning the letter with your cat's name rather than a nickname. You can always include the nicknames in the body of the letter. Using their given name allows you to have a conversation that is equal and respectful.

Then start telling your cat all those things that you brainstormed in your list, all those responses to the essential questions. If you find it is difficult to write just one letter, then do as many as you want.

The time that you spend on the letter is up to you. Some of my clients spend a little time writing each day. Some will write the entire letter in one sitting. No matter how you choose to write it, be sure to get the letter done. You will be so happy that you did.

Step 3 — Delivery

After your letter is written, go with your cat to a special place where you both are comfortable. I suggest you do this alone with your cat. That way you can give your companion full attention without worrying about others.

You love your cat. Take pleasure in the fact that you have a special bond and have written them a love letter. Sit on the couch or in a sunny spot near a window while you read it out loud to your cat, and feel good about how you are walking this journey of pet loss grief.

The end-of-the-chapter *Contemplation Questions* will give you more direction in writing and delivering the love letter to your beloved pet.

Chapter Wrap-Up

In this chapter, we talked about how writing a love letter helps you to feel deeper love and connection with your cat. Plus, it helps you to better manage your feelings of pet grief. I gave you the essential questions and other important aspects to consider when writing and delivering the love letter to your cat.

Please use the chapter's *Contemplation Questions* to further guide you through the process of writing and reading the love letter to your cat.

In the next chapter, you will get information on what you can expect after your cat reaches the end of life. You will learn how to plan for ways in which your life will be different and how to cope with these changes.

Chapter Thirteen Contemplation Questions

1. I shared with you some essential questions from my Rescue Joy from Pet Loss Grief program that help in laying the groundwork for writing your love letter. Is there anything that you can add that you want to tell your cat?

2. Do you have any feelings of pet grief while you write or when you read this letter to your cat?

3. What are you going to pay most attention to during this special time that you have with your cat?

14. Finding Compassionate Expectations

I totally understand that you are very sad and the last thing you want to think about is what to expect after your cat dies—while your cat is still living their last days, weeks, or months. I understand, and I am sad that you and your cat are going through such pain too. Even still, know that my goal is to continue to help you through this difficult time.

As with the other places I've described on your grief journey, it is essential that you prepare yourself for what is to come—whether that be the common and incorrect myths (chapter 4), the seven stages of grief (chapter 3), the insensitive comments from friends or family (chapter 5), determining when the time is right for the final day (chapter 12), or now—what to expect after the death of your cat. I want to give you as many tools as I can, so you feel supported throughout your journey and know what to expect.

Anticipation and preparation are essential to ensure your grief journey is one that includes grace and compassion along with the other common, but uncomfortable, feelings that come with loss.

Case Study — Hannah and Angel

Hannah found that by knowing what she was going to experience after Angel's death, she was able to navigate the challenges better. By knowing what to expect, she could deal with the multitude of changes in her life with more clarity and strength, and she could be present for Angel when Angel most needed her.

Hannah shared—

I really didn't want to plan ahead and be prepared for a different life after Angel. I wanted everything to stay the same. I figured if I didn't change anything— and if I purposely ignored the future, all would be okay.

Wendy, you helped me understand that it is not ridiculous to talk about how my life would be different after Angel died, even while Angel was still living.

You helped me to understand that planning ahead and determining what was going to happen is the best way to deal with my grief about losing Angel.

Even though I am not looking forward to the day when I make the decision to end Angel's life, I know what to expect. That takes away some of the fear and increases my own sense of power when considering the future.

Hannah's experience helped her understand how important it was to know what to expect. It helped her remember that her grief journey was unique to her, and it was also normal. With this knowledge she was able to proceed as she wished with her grieving experience.

Possible Experiences

Here are some of unexpected things that Hannah experienced that you may or may not experience after your cat dies.

You may become aware of . . .

- the different and unexpected changes in your life;

- the time when you really felt the full extent of your loss;

- the ways to redefine your relationship with your deceased cat;

- the new discoveries of some areas of personal growth through your pet grief; and/or

- the joyful memories of times you shared together.

Remember, this can be a very challenging time period for you. You will feel both the extent of your loss as well as the emergence of new feelings of grief. During this stretch of time, you will begin to recognize how your life is changing.

You are experiencing and learning who you are without your cat. You may move into a phase of discovering and understanding life without the physical presence of your cat.

You may spend time with new friends, have different adventures, or do things you always wanted to do but never did.

You may begin to think about getting another cat or volunteering at your local humane society.

You may even have some feelings of relief, which is perfectly normal. If your cat was very ill and suffered a lot during the end of their life, you may feel relieved that your cat is no longer suffering. This, too, is a natural feeling to have.

There are many things that will happen during this stage of pet loss grief, and they will be unique to you.

Please use the three *Contemplation Questions* at the end of the chapter to help you prepare for these changes and to establish the action plan that you can take to heal your pet grief.

Beautiful and Forever

There is no prescribed timeframe when you will experience these feelings, and you may not have these feelings at all. The relationship that you had with your cat is special to the both of you. And that will never change.

Your cat will live in your heart forever. This is a beautiful blessing that is private and special to the both of you. Those special moments sitting together at the sunny window, cuddled on the couch, and the love that you shared will never go away. Yet, your active grief will change over the days, weeks, months, and years after your cat dies, and something new will begin to develop.

The Metamorphosis of Grief

Another feeling that you may begin to recognize is more joy in your life. Please rest assured—it doesn't mean that you will no longer experience grief from the loss of your cat. It just means that you will begin to feel a shift in your awareness in regard to your grief. We will discuss this more in the next chapter.

When you are experiencing these changes in your life, you will be able to continue to acknowledge and honor your grief. Expect that your feelings of grief will resurface. Remember, that is common and very natural. But, you will be able to recognize and celebrate your growth and gains during this time as well!

No matter what your experience is during this time, continue to believe in your own process. Your grief is unique to you! It will continue to change, so it is important to reflect upon what you are going through.

Chapter Wrap-Up

As with the other parts of your grief journey, even after your cat passes, it is important to establish expectations and anticipate what your life may be like. In doing this, you are preparing yourself, which in turn helps you navigate your grief journey, including the time after your cat passes, with more grace, compassion, and grounding.

After your cat dies, you will begin to recognize some changes in your life that may seem out of place. And certain parts of your grief process will remain constant even though others will change.

In the next chapter, we explore happiness. I will show you that choosing happiness is part of the normal grieving process. You will learn that choosing happiness will not take away the forever bond you share with your cat. You will learn about your "new normal."

Chapter Fourteen Contemplation Questions

1. You learned the ways in which you can expect changes in your life after your cat reaches the end of life. Are there any expected changes that you anticipate you will experience?

2. Do you have any feelings of pet grief when recognizing these changes?

3. In regard to the changes that you expect for yourself after your cat dies, what are the ways in which you can prepare yourself so that you will feel supported?

15. Choosing Happiness

You might be thinking right now, while your cat is terminally ill, that it is simply wrong or impossible to contemplate feeling joy or happiness in the future. In fact, you may even think it is ridiculous to consider. Maybe you are asking why I am even bringing it up.

For now, please consider that this is something for you to be prepared for. Even though you are feeling intense grief right now, there will be a time when you will feel joy and happiness again.

Joy may be the last thing on your mind, and that is okay. As with other steps in your grief journey, anticipating and preparing for what is to come is essential, so that's why we need to map out this step, the step of choosing happiness.

Section Three Quick Recap

In this final section of *My Cat is Dying: What Do I Do?* you explored some very difficult and challenging issues that you may or may not be ready for. Awareness of these things is a crucial element in your successful navigation of the pet loss journey.

In this third section, you have been given tools for coping with your cat's illness. Section 3 has offered you ways to prepare as best you can for your cat's last day in their cycle of life. By preparing for this final day, you can find calm and clear-headedness amidst the chaos. Plus, we addressed how preparing for the making of tough decisions early on can help you gain even greater connection to the love that you feel for your cat.

You wrote a beautiful love letter to your cat, thanking them for the life that you both shared. This letter is another way in which you can tell your cat how much you love and appreciate them.

In the previous chapter, I helped you with some changes you may undergo when your cat reaches the end of life. We talked about how you will begin to recognize changes in yourself that may seem out of place. We also talked about how certain parts of your grief process will remain constant even though other parts will change.

Now I am going to share even more support tools that will guide you on how to rescue joy after your cat dies.

Preparing for Your "New Normal"

Even though your cat has not reached the end of life, it is important to be aware of the changes that will eventually occur, changes around you and within you.

Keep in mind that during this time period, expectations are going to increase from the people around you. This will be the time when you will begin to live your life differently than you did previously, and some people may not understand that.

This period does take time to adjust to, and we touched on it some in the previous chapter. I referred to it as your "new normal." In your "new normal," please be aware that you may experience both feelings of relief and possibly joy, both of which you may not have anticipated you'd feel. Because feeling relief and joy at this stage on your journey of grief can be unexpected, and possibly even unsettling, I want to offer you guidance, so you can move through this "new normal" with grace and compassion for yourself.

Even though your cat has not reached the end of life yet, being prepared for these feelings and how people are going to react to you is important.

Here is how a "new normal" can be described:

When you lose someone or something significant in your life, whether it is a spouse, family member, cat, limb, etc., that loss creates a completely different way for you to live your daily life. In this case, when your cat is no longer there for you to depend on or for them to depend on you, it will be a difficult period of time because that void challenges you to develop a new identity for yourself, new daily routines—and more.

Case Study—Jude and Freeda

Jude was part of my Rescue Joy from Pet Loss Grief support program. Jude and I talked a lot about how to cope with life after Freeda died and her "new normal."

Jude had a rough time with the death of Freeda. Freeda had been her constant companion. They did everything together. When Jude was home, Freeda would follow her from room to room and oftentimes sit on top of the kitchen cabinets, supervising Jude when she cooked.

When Freeda died, Jude's world completely changed. She lost her best friend, work partner, and confidant. Jude felt that she would never be able to be happy again.

Jude confided—

> *Without Freeda in my life, I am very confused. I want her back in my life. I know it is natural to have feelings of relief and moments of happiness, but I feel very discourteous to Freeda when I do. I can't even go into the kitchen and create beautiful food dishes that Freeda always had an opinion about. Plus, my friends think I am taking this to ridiculous levels, and someone even said that I was crazy to feel the way I do.*

Here is the thing about what Jude was experiencing—everything that she said is considered *normal grief*. She was experiencing a very huge loss in her life. For her to be able to articulate her grief as she did was very healthy.

Five Steps for Discovering Your "New Normal"

When Jude was ready, I shared with her the following five steps for discovering her "new normal." Hopefully they will help you with what you are experiencing as well.

1. A New Identity

While your cat is ill and you are preparing for the end of their life, your normal routines change. You are not the same person, and your normal activities with your cat are shifting and may even be gone.

Then when your cat has died, you no longer have a physical relationship with your cat. And you may never be the same as you were before your cat died.

Your self-identity will naturally change when your cat is ill and when they die. Jude experienced this with her love of cooking. Freeda was part of her inspiration and the creation of food dishes that Jude was known for. Without Freeda physically present Jude had to redefine her source of inspiration.

This is all part of the grief journey and something to keep in mind when planning out how you are going to create your new life. We will cover this more in *Book 4: My Cat Has Died:* **What Do I Do?** *Making Decisions and Healing the Trauma of Pet Loss.*

2. A New Relationship with Your Cat That Died

Many of my clients who are in my Rescue Joy from Pet Loss Grief program work on a common goal—not to forget their cat, but to change the relationship from a physical presence to one of wonderful memories or a spiritual relationship.

The checklist that you created in chapter 2 will help you stay on task so that you can spend quality time with your cat during their last weeks rather than always worrying that you didn't do enough or forgot to do something in regard to their care.

In your Comforting Routine List from chapter 7 and with the template to create your own list (that you downloaded in chapter 2), you will have many memories that will help you build a new relationship with your cat.

On the lists, you recorded what you did together, how your cat inspired you, silly things your cat did, and maybe even some things that you learned from your cat. These lists help preserve so many lovely memories, which now act as treasures to hold in your heart forever.

Plus, in chapter 13, you had a beautiful experience of writing a love letter to your cat, thanking your cat for all the wonderful things that they gave you.

By forming your new identity without your cat and allowing yourself to enjoy the many memories, you will begin to have a new relationship with your cat based on a different type of connection.

In *Book 4: My Cat Has Died*, we will talk more about creating a spiritual or nonphysical relationship with your cat so that you can continue to have a different type of bond with your beloved companion.

3. A New Group of Friends

Many people don't understand or respect the fact that losing a cat is painful. So many people think cats are independent and not in need of human contact. You know differently, and you may find that searching for new friends who are more supportive of you is important. For example, you may end up relying on and investing more time in the relationships with the people who were most supportive and nonjudgmental of you in your grief journey.

Also, if you were involved with any groups where you shared your love for cats, you developed friendships that included sharing the antics of your cats. Not having a cat right now can change the relationship that you have with these people.

You may feel left out or have the feeling that you can no longer relate to them.

4. A New Sense of Purpose

It is natural to question your purpose in life once your cat dies. Your cat made a difference in your life and depended on you. Now that your cat has died, you may be questioning the meaning of your current existence. This is common and normal.

Some people realize new life purposes and make significant life changes after their cats have died. For example, some decide to volunteer at their local humane societies, start cat rescue groups of their own, or start helping others with pet loss grief.

5. Celebration of Your Growth

When your cat dies, your journey of pet loss grief is life-altering. You didn't choose to experience the loss of your pet. Grief is usually unwanted or unplanned. However, the journey of grief is a wonderful experience for personal growth. Celebrate how you have grown from the opportunity to share life with your cat. Find joy in your growth and the lessons you have learned.

Some people learn through this experience how to be more sensitive to others going through the loss of their cats. Some decide to give back to cats in need. Some learn to celebrate the gifts that their cats gave them and live their lives fully with that in mind.

After Jude worked through these five steps and discovered a different way of dealing with her grief, she was able to celebrate her life with Freeda. She began to feel okay that she was starting to feel joy and happiness again.

Did her grief go away? No, it did not, but it changed.

Jude shared with me at the end of the Rescue Joy from Pet Loss Grief program—

> *I never thought it would be possible to be happy again without Freeda in my life. I thought that feeling happy would be disrespectful to Freeda. By exploring the five steps that you gave me, I was able to discover that what I was feeling was normal. I could still have feelings of happiness and joy amidst my grief.*

Even though you never forget your loss, you can learn different ways to live your life without your cat being physically with you.

Understanding that grief works in different ways can help you have an enriching experience and support your "new normal" as well. Please note that I will be offering even more ways to support your "new normal" in detail in the fourth book in *The Pet Bereavement Series* called *My Cat Has Died: What Do I Do? Making Decisions and Healing the Trauma of Pet Loss.*

Know that having an understanding of what happens to you after your cat dies will prepare you for the unexpected. Knowing what to expect and planning for it will help you rescue your joy from tremendous despair and dejection.

Having to say good-bye to your beloved cat is difficult. After all, you cat is your family and your best friend.

Your cat is here for only a short time compared to you, and the loss of a cat often brings up many feelings that are sometimes really difficult to deal with. That's why guidance, support, and preparation are so crucial to your successful navigation of the pet grief journey. That's why you've sought out *My Cat Is Dying: What Do I Do?*

Chapter Wrap-Up

Choosing happiness is part of the normal grieving process. Choosing happiness will not take away the forever bond that you share with your cat.

Please revisit the five steps for discovering your "new normal" to assist you in dealing with the fact that your cat is no longer physically with you.

Your journey with pet grief is unique to you and your cat. Honor your journey with respect and dignity for yourself and your companion. No one can alter that if you are aware of and accountable for your process.

Keep in mind that you shared your life with a wonderful creature. Now is your time to give that gift back to your cat. Allow yourself to feel the delight that your cat gave you.

Here are your last three *Contemplation Questions* that will help you rescue your joy from pet loss grief. Dedicate yourself to these questions only when you are ready.

Chapter Fifteen Contemplation Questions

1. In what ways has your cat shown you happiness in life?

2. What feelings of grief are you experiencing as you write down your feelings of joy and happiness?

3. Now that you understand that feeling joy and happiness is normal, can you list some of the ways in which you may be experiencing these feelings?

Final Thoughts

Your cat holds a special place in your heart that is endearing and healthy. You share daily routines, secrets, and quality time. Together you give each other a multitude of gifts that in some way make both of your lives a little easier and complete.

Your cat connects you to your own emotions and new ways of looking at life. They provide you with emotional nourishment that can be difficult to get from people.

Your cat clarifies for you the simple pleasures in life. In other words, they make you laugh and maybe persuade you to take things a bit less seriously.

Your beloved companion provides you with daily physical contact and comfort that is exclusive and particular to the relationship that you have with them.

Your cat pays attention to your secrets that no other person may even know. It is private and confidential, something that only the two of you completely understand.

It is, therefore, no surprise that when you get the news that your cat is dying, it creates some level of grief. This is vast and horrific news, and when something this significant is taken from your life, your entire world can change.

You can expect that you are going to feel sad, lonely, angry, hungry, not hungry, disoriented, and all the other normal feelings of grief.

Since your relationship with your cat is unique from that with anyone else, expect that your experience with pet loss grief is unique to you and your cat too. It all depends on your personality, your cat's personality, and your life experiences. What you experience will be completely different from that of someone else.

You are also going to experience that some people are just not going to get what you are going through. That is okay. It is not your job to change their opinions.

The important thing to do is to honor your cat, which you learned to do in this book and will learn more about in *Book 4: My Cat Has Died: What Do I Do? Making Decisions and Healing the Trauma of Pet Loss*. And, by all means, honor and trust yourself and the grief journey that you are walking. Surround yourself with friends, support groups, and a pet loss coach that will offer you support without judgment.

Remember to take care of yourself physically. If you are tired and feeling exhausted, you will not be able to be present for your cat and what they are experiencing. You are the caretaker now, and, by taking care of yourself, you will be able to give your cat the quality time that they deserve.

By planning ahead and anticipating things on your journey, you can be more present and loving for your cat and, in turn, experience more grace and compassion on this difficult and painful journey.

Your grief journey will not end when your cat dies. That is natural, common, and to be expected.

Resources

Ways in which I can support you

Center for Pet Loss Grief: Through Life, Death, and Beyond
Wendy Van de Poll, MS, CEOL

> https://centerforpetlossgrief.com

Best Selling and Award Winning Books
https://centerforpetlossgrief.com/books

> My Dog IS Dying: What Do I Do?
> My Dog HAS Died: What Do I Do?
>
> My Cat IS Dying: What Do I Do?
> My Cat HAS Died: What Do I Do?
>
> Healing A Child's Pet Loss Grief

Free Book
> Healing Your Heart From Pet Loss Grief

Free Pet Grief Support Kit
https://centerforpetlossgrief.com

Animal Mediumship
https://centerforpetlossgrief.com/animal-medium

Animal Communication
https://wendyvandepoll.com/animal-communication

Pet Funerals
https://centerforpetlossgrief.com/pet-funeral

Facebook
Center for Pet Loss Grief
https://facebook.com/centerforpetlossgrief

Pet Memorial Support Group
https://facebook.com/groups/petmemorials.
centerforpetlossgrief

Veterinarians:

Veterinary Medical Association
www.ahvma.org/

Home Euthanasia and Pet Hospice Veterinarians
www.iaahpc.org/

Online Product Support:

Herbal Support: Pet Wellness Blends Affiliate
www.herbs-for-life-3.myshopify.com/#_l_1e

Magnetic Therapy Supplies: aVivoPur Affiliate
www.avivopur.com/#_a_CenterForPetLossGrief

Heart in Diamonds: Affiliate
www.heart-in-diamonds.com/?aff=CenterForPetLoss

Support Groups:

Association for Pet Loss and Bereavement
www.aplb.org/

International Association for Animal Hospice and Palliative Care
www.iaahpc.org/

Association for Human-Animal Bond Veterinarians
www.aahabv.org/

Bereavement Book 4 in The Pet Series

My Cat Has Died: What Do I Do?

Making Decisions and Healing the Trauma of Pet Loss

Your cat was your best friend, and now that they are gone you are experiencing intense emotions that are making you feel uncomfortable.

It is critical to care for YOUR heart during this tough time and explore ways to help calm the chaos!

If you are feeling alone now that your cat has died, experiencing your friend's eyes glazing over when you cry, or your family, friends, and co-workers telling you to move on because it was only a cat, then this fourth book is for you.

After such a devastating loss, it is perfectly healthy to feel sad, angry, disoriented, depressed, etc. And it is not weird or silly to continue to seek out pet grief support. These feelings are just part of the necessary grieving stages to go through.

This book is for you if your cat has died and you are experiencing grief, having difficulty making important decisions, and you want to do something special to not forget the life you shared with your cat.

Plus, if you never want to lose the connection that you had with your cat and are looking for ways to have them spiritually in your life, you will find solutions in this book.

My Cat Has Died: What Do I Do? Making Decisions and Healing the Trauma of Pet Loss has been written to give you tools and options for navigating your personal journey through this raw and challenging time, a time filled with so many emotions and unexpected experiences. It is here as a handbook to keep with you as a constant guide to offer support in this particular phase of losing your cat.

My Cat Has Died: What Do I Do? will help you gain a deeper spiritual understanding of why your cat was in your life and to show you that even though they are not physically with you, your special and unique spiritual relationship with them will continue to grow. You will learn ways to talk to your cat, so you can experience their presence never completely leaving you.

You see—I know these feelings of grief very well as I have been there with many of my clients during their journeys. With each one, I am honored and humbled by the uniqueness of their relationship.

Your grieving process after the death of your cat is delicate, unique, and extremely important. When your beloved companion dies, this fourth book will support you through the final stages of grief and the mourning period as well. It can be an extremely difficult time—your life suddenly is not normal anymore because you lost your pet. It can take time to find a new normal.

Book 4 can help you with your grieving soul. Are you asking yourself some of the following questions now that your cat has died?

- Is what I am feeling really grief or am I going crazy?

- How do I deal with the hurtful things people are saying?

- How do I take care of myself now that my cat has died?

- How do I deal with my cat's body and should I arrange a funeral?

- How do I help my child with the loss of our family cat?

- Can I still communicate with my cat now that they are no longer physically with me?

My Cat Has Died: What Do I Do? will help you heal your soul and heart while dealing with the myriad feelings that will penetrate your daily life during this part of your journey.

Your cat was part of your life and your soul! The fear of death and beyond is natural. With continued growth and compassion for your journey, your heart will be full.

Acknowledgments

First, I want to thank all felines of the wild and those of the domesticated variety that "allow" us to share their living spaces. Your undying wisdom is uncanny and brilliant.

I would like to thank my clients who felt safe to express their grief stories with me so that I could write this book to help others: Sasha and Louie, Chloe and Cha-Cha, Heather and Tuxedo, Joanne and Gogger, Abigale and Moonlight, Linda and Ace, Donna and Snowflake, Marilyn and Bolt, Rachael and Avalanche, Norma and Babette, Kim and Bitsy, Carrie and Rosebud, Justine and Pine, Hannah and Angle, and Jude and Freeda.

To all the other fur, feather, and fin gurus who taught me those life lessons that as a human I may not want to deal with but must.

I am truly appreciative of the work done by my editor, Nancy Pile, who added her heart and paws to improve the book for your reading enjoyment.

I thank Debbie Lum who transforms my books with her formatting and Danijela Mijailovic for her beautiful cover designs.

A huge hug goes to my husband, Rick. His inspiration and support are always over-the-top amazing.

About the Author

Wendy Van de Poll is a pioneering leader in the field of pet loss grief support. Wendy is dedicated to providing a safe place for her clients to express their grief over the loss of their pets.

What makes Wendy successful with her clients is that she get's grief! *"Over the years I've dealt with my own grief and helping many families communicate and connect with their pets long after their loss. It's what I've done since I was just 5 yrs old!"*

She is compassionate and supportive to all who know her.

Her passion is to help people when they are grieving over the loss of a pet and her larger than life love for animals has led her to devote her life to the mission of increasing the quality of life between animals and people no matter what stage they are in their cycle of life! She has been called the animal whisperer.

She is a Certified End of Life and Pet Grief Support Coach, Certified Pet Funeral Celebrant, Animal Medium and Communicator. She is the founder of The Center for Pet Loss Grief and an international best selling and award-winning author and speaker.

She holds a Master's of Science degree in Wolf Ecology and Behavior and has run with wild wolves in Minnesota, coyotes in Massachusetts and foxes in her backyard. She lives in the woods with her husband, two crazy birds, her rescue dog Addie and all kinds of wildlife.

Wendy currently has a Skype, phone, and in person practice, providing end-of-life and pet grief support coaching, gentle massage and energy healing for animals, animal mediumship, and personalized pet funerals.

You can reach her at www.centerforpetlossgrief.com.

Thank You for Reading

My Cat Is Dying: What Do I Do?
Navigating Emotions, Decisions, and Options for Healing

Hello, I am a panther, and I work with Wendy when she connects with animals and their people on a spiritual level. Since this book is partly dedicated to me, it would mean a lot to all us felines, domesticated and wild, if you left a review on Amazon.

Felines are important to the work that Wendy does, and she honors their presence in her life every day.

We, felines, are happy that Wendy wrote this book so that she can help you on your pet loss journey. We would be grateful if you would leave a helpful REVIEW on Amazon:

Please go to this link: www.amzn.com/B01JGY1TKA to leave your review.

Thank you,

Panther

The Pet Bereavement Series
Best Selling and Award Winning Books

By Wendy Van de Poll, MS, CEOL

My Dog IS Dying: What Do I Do?
My Dog HAS Died: What Do I Do?

My Cat IS Dying: What Do I Do?
My Cat HAS Died: What Do I Do?

Healing A Child's Pet Loss Grief

Free Book

Healing Your Heart From Pet Loss Grief

CPSIA information can be obtained
at www.ICGtesting.com
Printed in the USA
BVHW051013050822
643886BV00003B/33

9 780997 375626